Chinese Astrology

孔子

Chinese Astrology

Paul Carus

Open Court
La Salle, Illinois

Publisher's Note

This 1974 Open Court Paperback edition is an abridged
version of a 1907 Open Court clothbound book entitled
Chinese Thought.

Carus, Paul, 1852-1919.
    Chinese astrology.

        Abridged version of the author's Chinese thought.
        1.   Astrology, Chinese. 2.   Philosophy, Chinese.
I.   Title.
BF1714.C5C35   1974   133.5   73-20411
ISBN   0-87548-155-8

Publisher's Preface

Chinese Astrology

Although Paul Carus wrote *Chinese Astrology* at the turn of the century its value continues to increase in three remarkable ways. First, it contains a lucid account of the major systems of Chinese mysticism up to the end of the 19th century. Most books currently available in the West concentrate on either Confucius or Lao Tze. Carus places these two spiritual and intellectual leaders in an historical continuum of ideas. The Yih System, P'an-Ku, Feng-Shu, Lo Pan, Joss Sticks—all mysterious puzzles—take their place in the history of Oriental thought. Also, Carus documents the Chinese appreciation of the ideogram as art and their love of aphorisms. Perhaps some of the puzzling features of modern China can be explained by noting the continuity of the forms of Chinese thought. Although the content of their aphorisms and enumeration system has been purged away, the same forms continue to bear their new ideas.

Secondly, Carus' unique work pictures Chinese astrology and western astrology side by side. Tables of symbols handily compare Chinese, Indian, Roman and Egyptian astrological concepts. Astrology's *aficionados* and sceptics will be fascinated by these puzzling similarities of symbols and will be drawn to wonder if there was more exchange between the East and West at the dawn of civilization than has been documented to date. Many of Carus' questions still await satisfactory answers: What is the relationship, historically and speculatively, between Leibniz' Binary System and Chinese mathematics? Is the Urim and Thummim of Jewish mysticism akin to Lao Tze's Yin-Yang? And, there are larger puzzles still incomplete: Was there a single "cradle of civilization"? A common origin of all zodiacs? If civilizations arose separately how can their striking similarities be explained? Which way did the tide of influence flow? Have some ideas returned to their home ports transformed by double sea-changes?

Thirdly, *Chinese Astrology* is a scholarly work that can take a proud place in the history of archaeology and Oriental studies. Consider the archaeological treasuretroves that came to light after the publication of Darwin's *Origin of the Species* in 1859. Troy's many layers were uncovered in 1871; Java Man was found in 1891; Flinders Petrie, the Grand Old Man of Egyptology, began his painstaking excavation of the Nagado cemetery in 1894; diggings in ancient Babylon were carried on from 1899-1914; and in 1900 Sir Arthur Evans discovered Knossos. All of these startling new finds were incorporated in Paul Carus' omnivorous search for knowledge. The methods of field-work and study now used by patient archaeologists and anthropologists were as important a product of the early scientific 20th century as the actual discoveries of prehistoric fragments. At the turn of the century, new theories were produced by laymen and scholars as rapidly as new gadgets were invented. It was up to Carus, as editor of a lively publishing house and two fortnightly magazines, to attend to all the purported facts and fancies that turned the 19th century into the 20th century; his role was to grant patents to those ideas worth the public's attention.

Phrases such as "There are three systems of religion authorized by the (Chinese) government," references to "the present Manchu dynasty," and assurances that "Pious people consult the oracle on all important occasions" fix the limits of this book. The oracle has changed, but the attitude? That is still a puzzle. Carus' scrupulous notes on what the well out-fitted Chinese use for divination will bring smiles. How things have changed! But Mao's China was not created *ex nihilo* and it is as true for the Middle Kingdom as for the rest of the world that understanding the present depends to a great extent on understanding the past. For China, this will entail finding out just exactly what it is that the Chinese people are now "free not to believe." While the Peking Man was discovered long after Dr. Carus' death, Peking People may still be discovered through Carus' work.

The depth and breadth of Carus' understanding is amazing. He never knew of the Olduvai Gorge or the Koster Corn Field in his home state of Illinois, but he was still far ahead of his time in his effort to comprehend non-western modes of thought, cultures and traditions. He did not have access to carbon dating, aerial photography and liquid latex for preserving inscriptions, but he approached every puzzle with a mind-freeing freshness, judiciously tempered by scientific method. He tried new combinations of puzzle pieces. He was always ready to acknowledge a hypothesis was, after all, merely hypothetical. Although many of his theories are out of date, Carus' curiosity and open scientific attitude should never be out of style. May excavations of artifacts from the 20th century be treated with such care and love of humanity!

—La Salle, Illinois 1974

TABLE OF CONTENTS.

CHINESE SCRIPT.

COMMUNICATION OF THOUGHT.

IN China the most ancient mode of recording thought was accomplished by *chieh shêng* (結繩) or "knotted cords," which is alluded to by Lao-Tze in his *Tao Teh King*, 道德經,[1] (written in the sixth century before Christ) as the ancient and venerable, though awkward, mode of writing, and also by Confucius in the third appendix to the *Yih King*.[2]

All detailed knowledge of the use of knotted cords in China has been entirely lost, but we can easily understand that it was a mnemo-technic method of remembering data of various kinds and communicating ideas. The same practice prevailed in ancient Peru as well as among the islanders of Oceania, and seems to have been common all over the globe among the peoples of a primitive civilisation.

In South America the knotted cords are called "quippu" and some that are still preserved in ethnological collections were used to indicate the tribute to be paid to the Incas by the several tribes. They consist of woolen threads, the different colors of which represent different kinds of produce: corn, wheat, fruits, furs, etc., while the number of knots register the amount or measure.[3]

---

[1] See *Lao-Tze's Tao Teh King*, Chapter 80.

[2] Section 23. See James Legge's translation in *Sacred Books of the East*, Vol. XVI, p. 385.

[3] What can be done with knotted strings is well illustrated by the fact that a string alphabet has been invented for the use of the blind in which the letters are indicated by form or arrangement. The knots are easily made

Herodotus informs us that King Darius when fighting the Scythians gave his orders to the Ionians in the form of a leathern thong with sixty knots in it, thereby indicating the number of days in which they should expect his return. We thus see that the Persians employed the same mnemo-technic means that have been discovered in several South Sea islands as well as in America, and we may assume that the ancient Chinese knotted cords (*chieh shêng*) also were in principle the same.

Knotted cords were replaced by notched bamboo sticks, and the incised characters may in olden times have been as primitive as are mnemotechnic communications of the American Indians, such as prayer-sticks and such other pictorial writings as are still extant.

*   *   *

The invention of writing in the proper sense of the word is credited to Ts'ang Hieh (蒼頡), also called Shih 'Huang (史皇), the "Record Sovereign" because he is the protector and patron saint of history and archival documents. He is said to have lived in the twenty-eighth century B. C., and having ascended a mountain overlooking the river Loh, he saw a divine tortoise rising from the water. It exhibited on its back mysterious tracings of letters which "lay bare the permutations of nature to devise a system of written records,"[6]—a report which imputes that he saw the characters of the five elements on the tortoise's back.

It is not impossible that Chinese writing has been introduced from ancient Mesopotamia, a theory vigorously advocated by M. Terrien de Lacouperie, rejected by many, but, after all, sufficiently probable to deserve serious consideration, for we cannot deny that many Chinese symbols exhibit a remarkable similarity to the ideograms of both ancient Babylonia and ancient Egypt, and remembering the fact that Chinese bottles have been discovered in Egyptian tombs and also in Asia minor, we cannot help granting that in prehistoric days there must have been more trade, and more travel, and a greater exchange of thought than is generally assumed.

---

and sufficiently different to be easily deciphered. The *Standard Dictionary*, II, p. 1780, contains an illustration of the string alphabet.

[6] Mayers's *Chinese Reader's Manual,* p. 228, I, No. 756.

We here reproduce from Garrick Mallery's work on *Picture Writing of the American Indians*,[7] a table of symbols which shows the cuneiform signs in three forms; pictorial, hieratic, and cursive, the Chinese and the Egyptian in parallel columns.

Pictorial	Hieratic	Cursive.	Chinese.	Egyptian	
					Sun.
					Hand.
					Fish.
					Corpse.
					Wood.
					Cave.
					Home.
					Place.
					Boundary
					God
					Ear.
					Water.
					Horn.
					Half.
					Door or Gate.

MALLERY'S TABLE.

A Comparison of the Cuneiform, Chinese, and Egyptian Systems of Writing.

The words omitted in the Chinese column of Mr. Mallery's

[7] *Ann. Rep. of the B. of Ethn.*, 1888-9, p. 675. Mr. Mallery does not state the source from which it is taken. It may be from W. St. Chad, Boscawen, or M. T. Lacouperie.

table (God, ear, home) are not less remarkable instances than the others.

The word "God" is more similar than it appears if we were to judge merely from its external shape. In cuneiform writing as well as in Egyptian it is a star, and the Chinese word *shih* (示) shows a horizontal dash and underneath three perpendicular wave lines. This seems very different from the Babylonian and Egyptian conceptions, but the Chinese character is explained to mean "light from the sky" or "celestial manifestation," the dash on top meaning "the heavens," and the three vertical lines depict the emanations in the form of rays.

The character for "ear," in its present form 耳 ('*rh*), might very well have originated from the Babylonian. The same is true of the Chinese character that denotes "field," or "farm land," which may very well be used in the sense of "homestead." The character *t'ien* (田) is in principle the same as the pictorial Babylonian and the hieroglyphic Egyptian.

Further, we have to add that the Chinese word meaning "corpse" is explained as "body lying" and thus resembles the Egyptian word for "mummy" which in different senses is represented either as a standing or a lying mummy.

We have to correct a mistake in Mr. Mallery's table; the word "half" in Chinese is not a cross, but either half a tree or the ideogram "cow" combined with the character "division." A cross means "completion" and the complete number of our fingers, viz. "ten."

Whether or not the theory of Lacouperie be tenable, one thing is sure, that all three systems of writing, the Babylonian, the Egyptian, and the Chinese, have begun with pictorial representations of the objects which, according to circumstances, were conventionalised in different ways.

The writing material always influences the character of a script. Thus, after the invention of brush and paper, the method of writing down from top to bottom was naturally retained, but the script acquired that peculiar picturesque character of brush dashes which it still possesses.

The hair brush is called *mao-pi*, or simply *pi* (bamboo pencil),* and tradition states that General Meng T'ien was the inventor of writing with a brush,—a statement which is not impossible but

| tortoise, | chariot, | child. | elephant, | deer, | vase, | hill, | eye |

| kwei, | chi, | tsz', | siang, | luh, | hu, | shan, | muh. |

PICTORIAL WRITING CONVENTIONALISED.†

strange, for he was the most faithful servant of Shih Hwang Ti, the great hater of ancient literature, who on capital punishment ordered all the ancient books burned. Shih Hwang was a warlike emperor who ruled from 259 until 210 B. C., and for the first time (in 222 B. C.) united the entire Chinese empire under one scepter. He is the same who erected the great wall, so expensive and at the same time so useless, and General Meng T'ien was in command of the laborers. When the Emperor died, General Meng T'ien is said to have committed suicide.[8]

We here reproduce a list of ornamental Chinese characters which are commonly, and without doubt rightly, assumed to represent the most ancient forms of Chinese writing with a brush.

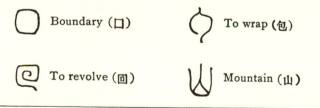

Boundary (口) To wrap (包)

To revolve (回) Mountain (山)

---

* The character 筆 *pi* consists of the radical "bamboo" and the word "brush" or "stylus."

† Reproduced from Williams's *Middle Kingdom*.

[8] See Mayers, *loc. cit.*, Nos. 597 and 497.

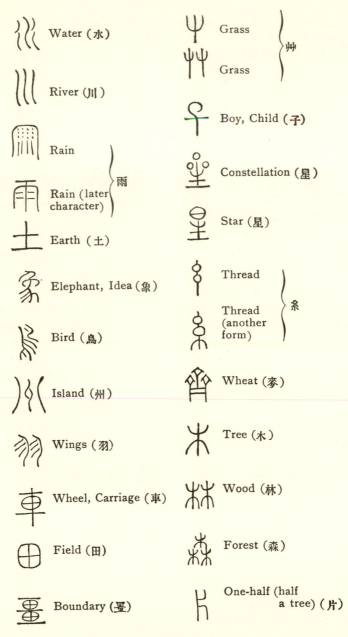

Water (水)

River (川)

Rain

Rain (later character) } 雨

Earth (土)

Elephant, Idea (象)

Bird (鳥)

Island (州)

Wings (羽)

Wheel, Carriage (車)

Field (田)

Boundary (畺)

Grass
Grass } 艸

Boy, Child (子)

Constellation (星)

Star (星)

Thread
Thread (another form) } 糸

Wheat (麥)

Tree (木)

Wood (林)

Forest (森)

One-half (half a tree) (片)

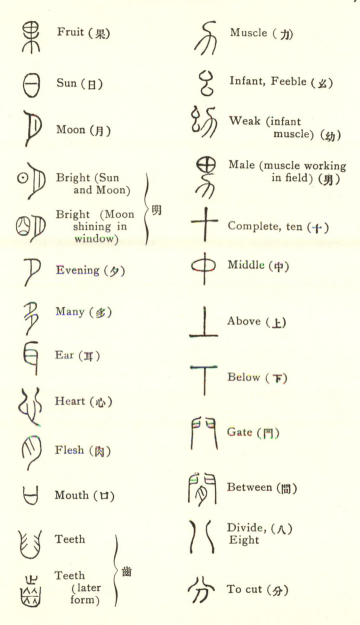

Fruit (果)

Sun (日)

Moon (月)

Bright (Sun and Moon)

Bright (Moon shining in window)

} 明

Evening (夕)

Many (多)

Ear (耳)

Heart (心)

Flesh (肉)

Mouth (口)

Teeth

Teeth (later form)

} 齒

Muscle (力)

Infant, Feeble (幺)

Weak (infant muscle) (幼)

Male (muscle working in field) (男)

Complete, ten (十)

Middle (中)

Above (上)

Below (下)

Gate (門)

Between (間)

Divide, Eight (八)

To cut (分)

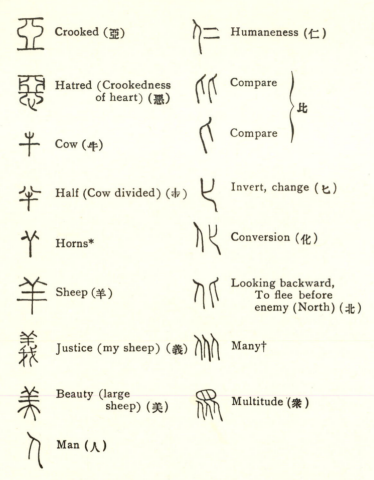

Crooked (亞)

Hatred (Crookedness of heart) (惡)

Cow (牛)

Half (Cow divided) (半)

Horns*

Sheep (羊)

Justice (my sheep) (義)

Beauty (large sheep) (美)

Man (人)

Humaneness (仁)

Compare

Compare

比

Invert, change (匕)

Conversion (化)

Looking backward, To flee before enemy (North) (北)

Many†

Multitude (衆)

Most of the symbols of the list explain themselves. A "boundary" is a simple line of enclosure. "Revolve" is a curve. The meaning of the signs "to wrap," "mountain," "water," "river," "rain," "horns," "grass," "child," "constellation" or "star," "thread," "wheat," "tree," "fruit," "sun," "moon," is obvious enough. The symbols "elephant," "bird," "heart" require more imagination; but

---

* This character does not exist in modern Chinese.
† Not used in modern Chinese.

the original picture is still recognisable in them. The word "flesh" is meant as a slice of meat. "Mouth," "teeth," "eye," are also intended to depict the objects. The word "muscle" represents the upper arm, and in connection with the word "weak" which originally means also "infant," it denotes "lack of strength." A character consisting of two lines, representing two pieces cut off, means "to divide." Later the character "knife," as the instrument by which the division is to be made, was added. Crooked roads mean "crooked" or "evil," and in combination with the word "heart" we have the word "hatred." In the symbol "cow" the horns form the most prominent part, the body being reduced to a mere cross. The symbol "cow" combined with the symbol "division" means "half." The picture of a sheep shows the symbol "horns" on the top while the rest is scarcely recognisable. The symbol "sheep" in combination with the symbol "mine" represents the character "justice," because the ancient Chinese were shepherds, and their main quarrels in courts of justice were disputes about the ownership of sheep; and their idea of beauty was expressed by "a sheep" that is "great." The symbol "middle" is easily understood and so are the symbols "below" and "above." The character "gate" is a picture of a double doorway, and the character "between" shows a mark between the two posts of the gate. The character "sun" or "moon" and a picture of a "window" means "bright," for if the moon shines into the window it denotes "brightness," and "sun and moon" in their combination mean the same, viz., the best light there is in the world. The ideogram "moon," if written in a special way, is read "evening," and if "moon" is repeated it means "many evenings," or simply "many." The earth is represented by a horizontal line on which a cross stands, implying that the soil of the earth is stable; it is the place on which to take a stand. Two trees mean "wood," three trees "forest." If the tree is cut in two, it originally denotes "one-half," later on it acquired the meaning "part or parcel," and finally "piece."

The outline map of a field means "field" or "farm," and lines limiting two fields mean "frontier" or "boundary."

If the character "man," of which only the legs are left, has the symbol "two" attached to it, it means the relation which obtains between two or several people, viz., "humanity," "humaneness," or "kindness." One man or two men turned the other way means "to compare." A man upside down means "to invert," "to change." One man in his normal position, and the other upside down acquires the sense of "transformation" or "conversion." One man in a normal position and another man looking the other way means "north," for the Chinese determine directions by looking south; hence, to look backward means "north." The symbol consisting of three men means "many." To this symbol is frequently attached the character "eye," and thereby it acquires the meaning "many as a unit," i. e., "a multitude."

A pretty instance of Chinese word formation is the word *shu* (書), which means "book" or "treatise," and is composed of the characters "brush" and "speak," the idea being that it is a thing in which "the brush speaks."

There are several styles of Chinese script (*shu*), and we here reproduce from Professor Williams's *Middle Kingdom* (Vol. II, p. 594) a table which shows at a glance their similarities and differences. The most old-fashioned style is called "the seal script," or, after the name of the inventor, *Chuen Shu*. The second is the official style, or *Lieh Shu,* used for engrossing documents and commonly considered the most elegant form of writing. The third is called the pattern or normal style (*Kiai Shu*) ; because it preserves most clearly the essential character of Chinese writing. The fourth is a shorthand and demotic style called cursive script or *Hing*[10] *Shu,* much used in practical life. It is the most difficult for foreigners to read, as many lines are run together, thus obliterating the distinctness of the original character. The fifth style is called the grass script or *Tsao Shu.* It is almost an approach to the easy hand of the Japanese, and its name may be translated "fancy style." Under the Sung dynasty a new style was adopted which is practically the same as the normal style, only showing more regularity, and it is

---

[10]*Hing* means "to walk," "to run"; and as a noun the same character means "element."

Sung style 6	Fancy style 5	Cursive style 4	Normal style 3	Official style 2	Seal style 1	
書	書	書	書	書	書	Writing
有	有	有	有	有	有	has
六	六	六	六	六	六	six
體	體	體	體	髀	體	styles,
曰	曰	曰	曰	曰	曰	viz.,
篆	篆	篆	篆	篆	篆	seal,
曰	曰	曰	曰	曰	曰	viz.,
隸	隸	隸	隸	隸	隸	official,
曰	曰	曰	曰	曰	曰	viz.,
楷	楷	楷	楷	楷	楷	normal,
曰	曰	曰	曰	曰	曰	viz.,
行	行	行	行	行	行	running or cursive,
曰	曰	曰	曰	曰	曰	viz.,
草	草	草	草	草	草	grass or fancy
曰	曰	曰	曰	曰	曰	viz.,
宋	宋	宋	宋	宋	宋	Sung.

SIX DIFFERENT STYLES OF CHINESE WRITING.
(Reproduced from Williams's *Middle Kingdom*.)

commonly called *Sung Shu* which has become the pattern of modern Chinese print.

The writing of Chinese requires eight different kinds of dashes, and the word *yung* (永), "eternal," contains all of them. This significant character accordingly has become the typical word with which Chinese scholars start their calligraphic lessons.

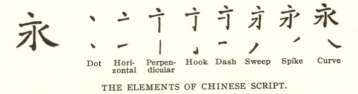

| Dot | Hori-
zontal | Perpen-
dicular | Hook | Dash | Sweep | Spike | Curve |

THE ELEMENTS OF CHINESE SCRIPT.

The little mark like a fat upward comma is called *dot*. Among the lines we have a *horizontal* and a *perpendicular*. Further there is a *hook,* which latter is added to the perpendicular by joining to its lower end a dot line. A *dash* is a short horizontal line. A tapering line downward is called a *sweep,* upward a *spike,* and a smaller sweep in the shape of a big downward comma, *stroke*. A crooked line is called a *curve.*

STOCK PHRASES AND STAPLE THOUGHTS.

The Chinese are in the habit of propounding their favorite notions and beliefs in enumerations. They are so accustomed to the mathematical conception of Yang and Yin that they would agree with Pythagoras who finds in number the explanation of the world.

The Chinese speak of the *liang i,* i. e., the two primary forms representing the positive and negative principles. Further they speak of the two great luminaries, sun and moon; the two divinities presiding over war and peace, the two emperors of antiquity, the two first dynasties, viz., the Hsia and Yin; and the two venerable men that hailed the advent of the Chow dynasty, etc.

The number "three" plays an important part in Chinese enumerations. There are three systems of religion authorised by the government: Confucianism, or the system of the Literati (儒); Bud-

dhism, or the system of Shakya Muni (釋); Taoism or the system
of Lao Tze (道). There are three kinds of heavenly light: of the
sun, the moon, and the stars. In Chinese ethics there are three
forms of obedience: of a subject toward his sovereign, of the son
toward his father, of a wife toward her husband. There are three
mental qualities (性) of a student: application (讀), memory (記),
understanding (悟). There are the three gems worshipped by
Buddhists, the Buddha, the Dharma, and the Sangha. There are

THE THREE GEMS OF BUDDHISM.

three pure ones or precious ones worshipped in the Taoist temples,
probably in imitation of the Buddhist trinity. There are three cere-
monial rituals; one in worshipping heavenly spirits, another in worshipping spirits of the earth, and the third one in worshipping the
spirits of ancestors. There are three sacrificial animals: the ox, the
goat, the pig. There are three holy men: Yao, Shun, and Yü.
There are three auspicious constellations: the constellation of happiness, the constellation of emolument, and the constellation of

longevity. There are three kinds of abundance that is desirable: abundance of good fortune, abundance of years, abundance of sons There are three powers (三 才) of nature: heaven (天), earth (地), man (人). There are three regions of existence, the heavens, the earth and the waters. There are three degrees of kinship. Further there are three penal sentences: the death penalty, corporeal punishment, and imprisonment. There are three tribunals of justice: the board of punishments, the court of judicature or appellate court, and the censorate or supreme court. There are three forms of taxation: land taxation, a service of twenty days labor each year, and tithes of the produce. There are three great rivers: the Yellow River, the Loh, and the I. There are three great river defiles: Kwang Tung, the Valley of the Yang Tse Kiang, and the defiles of the Si Ling on the Yellow River. There are three primordial sovereigns: Fuh Hi, Shen Nung, and Hwang Ti. In addition there are innumerable sets of three in the literature of the Confucianists, the Buddhists, the Taoists, and also in history.

The number "four" is not less frequent. We have four quadrants and four divisions of the heavens; the East is the division of the azure dragon, the North of the somber warrior, the South of the vermillion bird, and the West of the white tiger. There are four supernatural creatures considered as endowed with spirituality: *lin* (麟) or unicorn, *feng* (鳳) or phœnix, *kwei* (龜) or tortoise, and *lung* (龍) or dragon. The scholar possesses four treasures (寳): ink (墨), paper (紙), brush (筆), and ink slab (硯).[11] There are four figures which originate by combining the two primordial essences in groups of two, the great *yang,* the small *yang,* the great *yin* and the small *yin.* There are four cardinal points and four members of the human frame.

Instances of the number "five" are above all the five blessings (五 福): longevity (壽), riches (富), peacefulness (康) and serenity (寧), the love of virtue (攸 好 德), and a happy consummation of life (考 終 命). There are five eternal ideals (常): humaneness

---

[11] The Chinese have no ink stand but use a slab upon which they rub their ink, taking it as does a painter from a palette.

(仁), uprightness (義), propriety (禮), insight (智), and faith-fulness (信). There are five elements .(五 行): water, fire, wood, metal, earth. There are five cardinal relations among mankind: between sovereign and subject (君 臣), between father and son (父 子), between elder brother and younger brother (兄 弟), be-tween husband and wife (夫 婦), between friend and friend (朋 友). There are five genii: of spring, of summer, of mid-year, of autumn, and of winter. There are five beasts used for offerings: the ox, the goat, the pig, the dog, the fowl. There are five colors: black, red, azure, white, yellow. There are five classes of spiritual beings:

仁義禮智信　五常　　攸好德考終命　壽富康寧　五福

THE FIVE IDEALS.　　　THE FIVE BLESSINGS.

ghosts or disembodied human spirits, spiritual men, immortalised beings living in this world, deified spirits who have departed from the material world and live in the islands of the blest, and the celes-tial gods who enjoy perpetual life in heaven, There are five planets: Venus, Jupiter, Mercury, Mars, and Saturn. Further the Buddhists enumerate five attributes of existence: form, perception, conscious-ness, action, and knowledge. There are five degrees of feudal rank, five tastes, five notes of harmony in music, five sacred mountains, five kinds of charioteering, five colors of clouds, five ancient em-perors, five imperial courts, five kinds of mourning, etc., etc.

NORMAL STYLE.

GRASS STYLE.   A NEW YEAR'S CARD.*

THE CHARACTER "BLESSING."

五蝠

THE FIVE BATS.

(After a Tibetan picture.)

---

* The deity Wen Ch'ang points upward, indicating that all blessings come from heaven.

The characters which stand for the five blessings, and also the five eternal ideals, are naturally the most popular symbols all over China. They are used for congratulations and are inscribed upon wall pendants as ornaments. Among them the characters "longevity" and "blessing" are most used of all. They appear upon the decanters of convivial meetings; they are written on the bottom of tea cups; they are wrought into artistic forms of furniture; they

CHINESE SAUCER WITH PHOENIX AND DRAGON.
The centre contains the character *fu* "blessing."

are used for buckles, on pins, on dresses, and as ornaments of every description.

Blessing is called *fu* in Chinese, which is an exact homophone of *fu* meaning "bat," and so the five blessings, *wu fu,* are frequently represented by five bats.

The word "longevity" is commonly transcribed by *sheu.** and

* The diphthong *eu* in *sheu* is to be pronounced separately and in continental pronunciation, as English *ay* and with following *u*. Giles transcribes

means "old age, years, a long and prosperous life, birthday, to endure, forever," etc., and is also euphemistically used for "death."

The popularity of the word exceeds every other perhaps in any language, and the character is conspicuous in China everywhere and in innumerable variations.

As an instance of this tendency we reproduce the adjoined illustration, which is a photograph of the upper part of one of three tablets containing specimens of ornamental characters meaning *sheu,* "long life." The characters are over two inches in height, and are made of mother of pearl, in high relief, on a red background. On the three tablets there are altogether 180 different characters. The tablets belonged to the leader of the T'ai Ping, the Christian Chinese sect who rebelled against the present Manchu dynasty and were subdued with the assistance of General Gordon. They passed into the hands of Julius Saur, who was at that time a resident of Shanghai, when he went to Nanking, in company with Captain Fishborn, to treat for peace.

The meaning of the symbol "longevity" is not limited to the secular meaning of long life in this world, but is endowed with religious signification verging on the idea of immortality among Western peoples.

---

the word *shou.* The character consists of radical 33 (pronounced *see,* i. e., "scholar") and eleven additional strokes made up of the words "old," "to speak" and "word."

The star of longevity is Canopus, which is a of Argo.

Ancient traditions tell us that Si Wang Mu, the Royal Mother of the West, who lives in the Kwun Lun Mountains, possesses a peach-tree bearing fruit but once in three thousand years. From the

THE LONGEVITY SYMBOL IN DIFFERENT STYLES.

peaches of this tree the elixir of life can be distilled, and this is the reason why the peach symbolises longevity. Other symbols of longevity are the pine-tree, the crane, and the tortoise.*

* For special reference see De Groot's *Religious Systems of China*, pp. 56-57.

Of enumerations in sets of six we will only mention the six accomplishments: intelligence, humanity, holiness, sincerity, moderation (keeping the middle path), and benignity; further the six forms of writing: the seal character, the ancient official style, the normal style, the cursive style, the grass style, and the printer's style.

There are fewer enumerations of seven than might be expected. We mention the seven sages in the bamboo grove, the seven precious things (Sapta Ratna) of the Buddhists, the seven primary

THE CHARACTER 樂 ON CUFF BUTTON.   LONGEVITY PIN.

notes of music, the seven stars of Ursa Major commonly called "the dipper," the seven apertures of the head: ears, eyes, nostrils, and mouth; the seven luminaries: sun, moon, and the five planets; the seven emotions: joy, anger, grief, fear, love, hatred, desire.

The most important set of eight is the eight *kwa* or trigrams.

The figure "nine" is represented as the nine heavens, situated, one in the center, and the eight remaining ones in the eight divisions of the compass. There are further nine degrees of official rank, and nine divisions of the Great Plan, an ancient Chinese state document.

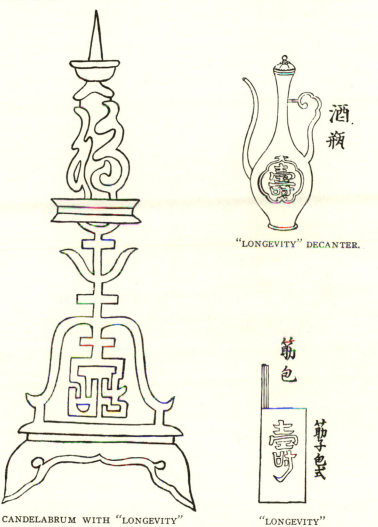

CANDELABRUM WITH "LONGEVITY"
AND "HAPPINESS" SYMBOLS.

"LONGEVITY" DECANTER.

"LONGEVITY"
CHOPSTICK HOLDER.

There are ten canonical books: the Book of Changes, the Book of History, the Book of Odes, the Record of Rites, the Ritual of the

Chow Dynasty, the Decorum Ritual, the Annals of Confucius, the Three Commentaries, the Conversations of Confucius (*Lun Yü*), and the Book of Filial Piety. There are ten commandments and ten heinous offences.

Of twelve we have the twelve animals of the duodenary cycle called rat, ox, tiger, hare, dragon, serpent, horse, goat, monkey, cock, dog, and pig. They preside, each one over a special hour of the day and the night and are supposed to exercise an influence peculiar to the character of the several animals. There are further

BUCKLE WITH CHARACTERS "LONGEVITY" AND "BLESSING."

twelve months, corresponding to the twelve divisions of the ecliptic, and the Buddhists speak of the twelve Nidanas or links in the chain of causation.

The figure "twenty-eight" is important as the number of days of a lunar month. Accordingly, the heavens are divided into twenty-eight constellations or stellar mansions, and it is noteworthy that four days in the twenty-eight, corresponding to the Christian Sunday, have been signified as resting-days and are denoted by the character *mi* (密 日) which has been traced to the Persian Mithra and proves that, in remote antiquity, Mithraism must have exercised an influence upon Chinese habits.[12]

CRANE AND TORTOISE.*
Symbols of long life. (Bronze candlestick.)

These enumerations are not accidental and indifferent notions, but form the staple thoughts of Chinese ethics. They have become

[12] See Mr. A. Wylie's article on the subject in the *Chinese Recorder,* Foo Chow, June and July numbers, 1871.

* The tortoise drags along the moss that has grown on its back.

fundamental principles of Chinese morality and constitute the back-
bone of the convictions of every half-way educated inhabitant of
China. Whatever their station in life may be, all Chinese people
know these ideas, they bear them in mind and allow their lives to
be determined by the conception of the five eternal ideals, the five
virtues, the five blessings, etc. They recognise in nature the funda-

THE LONGEVITY GARMENT.*

mental contrast of Yang and Yin as having originated from the
great origin and believe that the moral world of social conditions
is governed by the same law. Their highest ambition is to fulfil
all the demands of *hsiao,* i. e., "filial piety." Scholarship is highly
respected, and even the lower classes are punctilious in the observance of all rules of propriety.

---

* Reproduced from Professor De Groot's *Religious Systems of China,*
page 60.

CHINESE OCCULTISM.

BELIEF in mysterious agencies characterises a certain period in the religious development of every nation. Even the Jews, distinguished among the Semites by their soberness, consulted Yahveh through the Urim and Thummim, an oracle the nature of which is no longer definitely known. Kindred institutions among most nations are based upon primitive animism, or a belief in spirits, but in China we have a very peculiar mixture of logical clearness with fanciful superstitions. Chinese occultism is based upon a rational, nay a philosophical, or even mathematical, conception of existence. An original rationalism has here engendered a most luxurious growth of mysticism, and so the influence of occultism upon the people of the Middle Kingdom has been prolonged beyond measure.

THE YIH SYSTEM.

Among the ancient traditions of China there is a unique system of symbols called the *yih* (易), i. e., "permutations" or "changes,"

THE TWO PRIMARY FORMS* (LIANG I).

	THE YANG	THE YIH
Old form	○	●
Modern form	▬▬	▬ ▬

* It is difficult to translate the term *Liang I*. One might call the two *I* "elements," if that word were not used in another sense. The two *I* are commonly referred to as "Elementary Forms" or "Primary Forms." De Groot speaks of them as "Regulators."

which consists of all possible combinations of two elements, called *liang i* (兩 儀), i. e., the two elementary forms, which are the negative principle, *yin* (陰), and the positive principle, *yang* (陽). The four possible configurations of yang and yin in groups of two are called *ssu shiang* (四 象), i. e., "the four [secondary] figures"; all further combinations of the elementary forms into groups of three or more are called *kwa* (卦). In English, groups of three elementary forms are commonly called trigrams, and groups of six, hexagrams.

The book in which the permutations of yang and yin are recorded, was raised in ancient times to the dignity of a canonical writing, a class of literature briefly called *king* in Chinese. Hence the book is known under the title of *Yih King*.

The *Yih King* is one of the most ancient, most curious, and most mysterious documents in the world. It is more mysterious than the pyramids of Egypt, more ancient than the Vedas of India, more curious than the cuneiform inscriptions of Babylon.

In the earliest writings, the yang is generally represented as a white disk and the yin as a black one; but later on the former is replaced by one long dash denoting strength, the latter by two short dashes considered as a broken line to represent weakness. Disks are still used for diagrams, as in the Map of Ho and the Table of Loh, but the later method was usually employed, even before Confucius, for picturing kwa combinations.

The trigrams are endowed with symbolical meaning according to the way in which yin and yang lines are combined. They apply to all possible relations of life and so their significance varies.

Since olden times, the yih system has been considered a philosophical and religious panacea; it is believed to solve all problems, to answer all questions, to heal all ills. He who understands the yih is supposed to possess the key to the riddle of the universe.

The yih is capable of representing all combinations of existence. The elements of the yih, yang the positive principle and yin the negative principle, stand for the elements of being. Yang means "bright," and yin, "dark." Yang is the principle of heaven; yin, the principle of the earth. Yang is the sun, yin is the moon. Yang is masculine and active; yin is feminine and passive. The

THE FOUR FIGURES (SSU SHIANG).

SYMBOL	NAME	SIGNIFICANCE					
☰	Yang Major	Sun	Heat	Mentality (or leader-ship)	Unity (or origin)	The nature of things (essence)	Eyes	Great Monarch[3]
☳	Yang Minor	Fixed Stars	Day-light	Corporality (bodily organism)	Rotation	Compound things[1]	Nose	Prince
☵	Yin Minor	Planets	Night	Materiality (inertia; bodily substance)	Succession	Multiplicity[2]	Mouth	Duke
☷	Yin Major	Moon	Cold	Sensuality; passion	Quality	Attributes of things	Ears	Emperor

[1] Unity in multiplicity, i. e., the Yang dominating over the Yin.
[2] Multiplicity in unity, i. e., the Yin dominating over the Yang.
[3] While the Yin major denotes dominion in the concrete world of material existence, the Yang major symbolises the superhuman and supernatural, the divine, the extraordinary, such as would be a genius on a throne, a great man in the highest sense of the word.

former is motion; the latter is rest. Yang is strong, rigid, lordlike; yin is mild, pliable, submissive, wifelike. The struggle between, and the different mixture of, these two elementary contrasts, condition all the differences that prevail, the state of the elements, the nature of things, and also the character of the various personalities as well as the destinies of human beings.

The *Yih King* (易 經) is very old, for we find it mentioned as early as the year 1122 B. C., in the official records of the Chou dynasty, where we read that three different recensions of the work

THE EIGHT KWA FIGURES AND THE BINARY SYSTEM.

NAME	TRANSCRIP-TION	MEANINGS OF THE CHINESE WORD*	KWA	BINARY SYSTEM	ARABIC NUMERALS
乾	ch'ien	to come out; to rise, sunrise; vigorous; (present meaning) dry.		111	7
兌	tui	to weigh; to barter; permeable.		110	6
離	li	to separate.		101	5
震	chan	to quake; to thunder.		100	4
巽	sun	peaceful; a stand or pedestal.		011	3
坎	k'an	a pit; to dig a pit.		010	2
艮	kan	a limit; to stop; perverse.		001	1
坤	kw'un	earth; to nourish; yielding.		000	0

*A native student of the Yih system does not connect the usual meaning of the word with the names of the eight Kwas, and we insert here a translation of the character only for the sake of completeness.

were extant, the *Lien Shan,* the *Kwei Ts'ang* and the *Yih of Chou,*[1] of which, however, the last one alone has been preserved.

This *Yih of Chou,* our present *Yih King,* exhibits two arrangements of the kwa figures, of which one is attributed to their origi-

[1] Lien Shan means "mountain range" and by some is supposed to be a *nom de plume* of Shen Nung (i. e. "divine husbandman"), the mythical ruler of ancient China (2737-2697 B. C.), successor to Fuh-Hi. Others identify Lien Shan with Fuh-Hi. Kwei Ts'ang means "reverted hoard" and may have been simply an inversion of the Lien Shan arrangement. Its invention is assigned to the reign of Hwang Ti, "the Yellow Emperor," the third of the three rulers, (2697-2597 B. C.), a kind of a Chinese Numa Pompilius. The Chou redaction of the *Yih,* which is the latest one, is named after the Chou dynasty.

nator, the legendary Fuh-Hi,[2] the other to Wen Wang.[3] Fuh-Hi is also called Feng,[4] "wind," and Tai Ho,[5] "the great celestial," and he lived, according to Chinese records, from 2852 to 2738 B. C.

It speaks well for the mathematical genius of the ancient founders of Chinese civilisation that the original order of the yih, attributed to Fuh-Hi, corresponds closely to Leibnitz' Binary System of arithmetic. If we let the yin represent 0 and the yang, 1, it appears that the eight trigrams signify the first eight figures from 0-7, arranged in their proper arithmetical order, and read from below upward. Leibnitz knew the yih and speaks of it in terms of high

FUH-HI.

appreciation. Indeed it is not impossible that it suggested to him his idea of a binary system.

While Fuh-Hi's system exhibits a mathematical order, Wen Wang's is based upon considerations of occultism. It stands to reason that Fuh-Hi (by which name we understand that school, or founder of a school, that invented the yih) may not have grasped the full significance of his symbols in the line of abstract thought and especially in mathematics, but we must grant that he was a

---

[2]伏羲　　　[3]文王　　　[4]風　　　[5]太昊

mathematical genius, if not in fact, certainly potentially. As to further details our information is limited to legends.

The case is different with Wen Wang, for his life is inscribed on the pages of Chinese history and his character is well known.

The personal name of Wen Wang (i. e., the "scholar-king") is Hsi-Peh, which means "Western Chief." He was the Duke of Chou, one of the great vassals of the empire, and lived from 1231 to 1135 B. C. In his time the emperor was Chou-Sin, a degenerate debauché and a tyrant, the last of the Yin dynasty, who oppressed the people by reckless imposition and provoked a just rebellion. Wen Wang offended him and was long kept in prison, but his son

THE TRIGRAMS AS FAMILY RELATIONS.

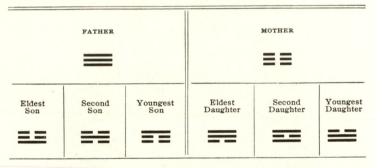

Fa, surnamed Wu Wang, being forced into a conflict with Chou-Sin, overthrew the imperial forces. The tyrant died in the flames of his palace which had been ignited by his own hands. Wu Wang[6] assumed the government and became the founder of the Chou dynasty which reigned from 1122 until 225 B. C.

Wen Wang was a man of earnest moral intentions, but with a hankering after occultism. During his imprisonment he occupied himself in his enforced leisure with the symbols of the yih, and found much comfort in the divinations which he believed to discover in them. When he saw better days he considered that the

---

[6] Wu Wang was born 1169 B. C.; he became emperor in 1122 B. C. and died 1116 B. C.

prophecies were fulfilled, and his faith in their occult meaning became more and more firmly established.[7]

The eight permutations of the trigrams apparently form the oldest part of the *Yih King*. They have been an object of contemplation since time immemorial and their significance is set forth in various ways. The trigrams consisting of three yang lines are called the unalloyed yang, and of three yin lines, the unalloyed yin. In the mixed groups the place of honor is at the bottom, and if they are conceived as family relations, the unalloyed yang represents

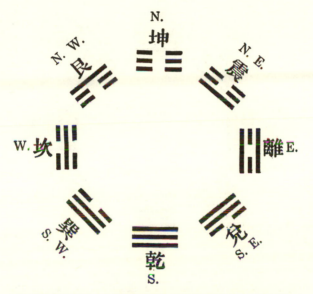

ARRANGEMENT OF TRIGRAMS ACCORDING TO FUH-HI.

the father and the unalloyed yin, the mother. The three sons are represented by the trigrams containing only one yang; the eldest son having yang in the lowest place, the second in the middle, and the third on top. The corresponding trigrams with only one yin line represent in the same way the three daughters.

The trigrams are also arranged both by Fuh-Hi and Wen Wang in the form of a mariner's compass. In the system of Fuh-Hi the

---

[7] Mayers, *Chinese Reader's Manual,* p. 177.

unalloyed yin stands at the north, the unalloyed yang at the south.
The others are so arranged that those which correspond to 1, 2, 3,
of Leibnitz' Binary System proceed from north through west to
south in regular order, while 4, 5, 6, start from south taking the
corresponding places in the east. In this mathematical arrangement we always have the opposed configurations in opposite quarters,
so as to have for each place in every opposite kwa a yang line correspond with a yin line and *vice versa;* while if they are expressed

ARRANGEMENT OF TRIGRAMS ACCORDING TO WEN WANG.

in numbers of the binary system, their sums are always equal to
seven.

Wen Wang rearranged the trigrams and abandoned entirely
the mathematical order attributed to Fuh-Hi. The following quo-
tation from the *Yih King* evinces the occultism which influenced
his thoughts:

"All things endowed with life have their origin in chan, as chan corresponds to the east. They are in harmonious existence in siuen because siuen
corresponds to the southeast. Li is brightness and renders all things visible

to one another, being the kwa which represents the south. Kw'un is the earth from which all things endowed with life receive food. Tui corresponds to mid-autumn. Ch'ien is the kwa of the northwest. K'an is water, the kwa of of the exact north representing distress, and unto it everything endowed with life reverts. Kan is the kwa of the northeast where living things both rise and terminate."

Since this new arrangement is absolutely dependent on occult considerations, the grouping must appear quite arbitrary from the standpoint of pure mathematics. It is natural that with the growth of mysticism this arbitrariness increases and the original system is lost sight of.

The yin and yang elements are supposed to be the product of a differentiation from the *t'ai chih,* "the grand limit," i. e., the absolute or ultimate reality of all existence, which, containing both yang and yin in potential efficiency, existed in the beginning. The grand limit evolved the pure yang as ether or air, which precipitated the Milky Way, shaping the visible heaven or firmament; while the yin coagulated and sank down to form the earth. But the earth contained enough of the yang to produce heat and life. Some unalloyed yang particles rose to form the sun, while correspondingly other unalloyed yin particles produced the moon, the two great luminaries, which in their turn begot the fixed stars.

THE TABLET OF DESTINY.

At the beginning of Chinese history stands a tablet which in some mysterious way is supposed to be connected with an explanation of the universe. It has been reconstructed by later Chinese thinkers and is pictured in the hands of Fuh-Hi as an arrangement of the kwa figures preserved in the *Yih King.* Considering the several traces of Babylonian traditions in ancient Chinese literature and folklore, would it not be justifiable to identify the tablet of Fuh-Hi with the ancient Babylonian "Tablet of Destiny" mentioned in the Enmeduranki Text, a copy of which was discovered in the archives of Asurbanipal[20] and was said to contain the "Mystery of Heaven and Earth?"

---

[20] K2486 and K4364; cf. Zimmern, KAT³ 533.

Enmeduranki, king of Sippar, is the seventh of the aboriginal kings, and he declares that he received the divine tablet "from Anu, [Bel, and Ea]."[21]

Chinese sages have their own interpretation of the phrase "the mystery of heaven and earth." They would at once associate the words "heaven" and "earth" with the two opposing principles yang and yin, and the question is whether among the ancient Sumerians there was not a similar tendency prevalent. It seems to be not impossible that the Chinese tablet in the hands of Fuh-Hi is the same as the "Tablet of Destiny" of the Sumerians, and when some Assyriologist has informed himself of the primitive Chinese conception of this mysterious tablet, he may be able to throw some additional light on the subject.

DIVINATION.

An explanation of the universe which derives all distinctions between things, conditions, relations, etc., from differences of mixture, must have appeared very plausible to the ancient sages of China, and we appreciate their acumen when we consider that even to-day advanced Western scientists of reputation attempt to explain the universe as a congeries of force-centers, acting either by attraction or repulsion in analogy to positive and negative electricity. On the ground of this fact the educated Chinese insist with more than a mere semblance of truth, that the underlying idea of the Chinese world-conception is fully borne out and justified by the results of Western science.

While it is obvious that the leading idea of the yih is quite scientific, we observe that as soon as the Chinese thinkers tried to apply it *a priori* without a proper investigation of cause and effect, they abandoned more and more the abstract (and we may say, the purely mathematical) conception of the yang and yin, fell victims to occultism, and used the yih for divination purposes. When we compare the vagaries of the occultism of the yih with the accom-

---

[21] Anu, Bel, and Ea are the Sumerian trinity. The words Bel and Ea are illegible on the tablet and have been restored by an unequivocal emendation. A doubtful word of the tablet has been translated by "omen" which presupposes that the translator regards the tablet as a means of divination.

plishments of Western science, we may feel very wise and superior, but we should not forget that it was the same fallacious argument of wrong analogy which produced in China the many superstitious practices of the yih, and in the history of our civilisation, astrology, alchemy, and magic. These pseudo-sciences were taken seriously in the world of thought throughout the Middle Ages and began to be abolished only after the Reformation with the rise of genuine astronomy, genuine chemistry, and genuine nature science. If the

A DIVINATION OUTFIT.

Chinese are wrong we must remember that there was a time when we made the same mistake.

The Chinese outfit for divination consists of fifty stalks called "divining-sticks" and six small oblong blocks to represent the hexagrams. These blocks are not unlike children's building-blocks, but they bear on two adjoining sides incisions dividing the oblong faces into equal sections, so as to give the surface the appearance of a yin figure. The sticks are made of stalks of the milfoil plant (*ptarmica sibirica*) which is cultivated on the tomb of Confucius and regarded as sacred.

Pious people consult the oracle on all important occasions. They are first careful to make themselves clean, and then assume a calm and reverential attitude of mind. The diviner then takes out one stick and places it in a holder on the center of the table. This single stalk is called "the grand limit" (*t'ai chih*), the ultimate cause of existence. He next lifts the forty-nine remaining sticks above his forehead with his right hand, and divides them at random into two parts, at the same time holding his breath and concentrating his thoughts on the question to be answered. The sticks in the right hand are then placed on the table, and one is taken out from them and placed between the fourth and fifth fingers of the left hand. The three groups are now called heaven, earth and man. The left-hand group is then counted with the right hand in cycles of eight, and the number of the last group yields the lower trigram of the answer, called the inner complement. This number is counted after the oldest order of the eight trigrams, viz., that of Fuh-Hi corresponding to the inverted binary arrangement. The upper trigram, called the outer complement, is determined in the same way.

After the hexagram is determined, one special line is selected by the aid of the divining-sticks in the same way as before, except that instead of counting in cycles of eight, the diviner now counts in cycles of six. Having thus established the hexagram and a special line in it, he next consults the *Yih King* which contains a definite meaning for each hexagram as a whole, and also for each single line; and this meaning is made the basis of the divine answer.

It is obvious that this complicated process presupposes a simpler one which, however, must have been in use in pre-historic times, for as far as Chinese history dates back the divining stalks and the kwa system are referred to in the oldest documents.

URIM AND THUMMIM.

The Chinese method of divination may help us to understand the Urim and Thummim of the Hebrews which are so ancient that details of their method are practically forgotten.

We notice first that the Urim and Thummim are two sets of symbols apparently forming a contrast similar to that of yin and yang. It is not probable that they were a set of twelve gems representing the twelve tribes of Israel. Secondly, like the yin and yang, the two sets must have been a plurality of elements and not only two symbols as is sometimes assumed; and thirdly, they served the purpose of divination, for they are referred to in connection with the ephod which must have had something to do with the determining oracle.

The Urim and Thummim* are translated in the Septuagint† by "manifestation and truth," or, as it has been rendered in English, "light and perfection." It appears that the vowel in the first word is wrong, and we ought to read *Orim,* which is the plural form of *Or,* "light," and might be translated by "the shining things." If Thummim is to be derived from the root THAMAM, its vocalisation ought to be *thamim* (not *thummim*) and would mean "the completed things."

We cannot doubt that the Urim and Thummim form a contrast, and if the Urim represent "light" or yang, the Thummim would represent "darkness" or yin, the former being compared to the rise of the sun, the latter to the consummation of the day.

Sometimes the answer of the Urim and Thummim is between two alternatives (as in 1 Sam. xiv. 36 ff), some times a definite reply is given which would presuppose a more or less complicated system similar to the answers recorded in the *Yih King.* In the history of Saul (1 Sam. x. 22) the answer comes out, "Behold, he hath hid himself among the stuff," and in the time of the Judges (Judges xx. 28) the question is asked about the advisability of a raid against the tribe of Benjamin, and the oracle declares, "Go up; for to-morrow I will deliver them into thine hand." On other occasions the oracle does not answer at all,‡ and its silence is interpreted as due to the wrath of God.

The answer received by consulting the Urim and Thummim was regarded as the decision of God, and was actually called the voice of God. This view seems to have led in later times, when the process of divination was no longer understood, to the assump-

---

* הָאוּרִים וְהַתֻּמִּים   † δήλωσις καὶ ἀλήθεια.

‡ See Sam. xiv. 37 and xxviii. 6.

tion that Yahveh's voice could be heard in the Holy of Holies, a misinterpretation which is plainly recognisable in the story of the high priest Eleazar (Num. vii. 89).

The Urim and Thummim are frequently mentioned in close connection with the ephod which has been the subject of much discussion. It is commonly assumed that the word is used in two senses, first as an article of apparel and secondly as a receptacle for Urim and Thummim. Unless we can find an interpretation which shows a connection between the two, we can be sure not to have rightly understood the original significance of this mysterious article. The description of the ephod in Exodus ii. 28, (an unquestionably postexilic passage) is irreconcilable with the appearance, use or function which this curious object must have possessed according to our historical sources, and the latter alone can be regarded as reliable. After considering all the passages in which the ephod is mentioned we have come to the conclusion that it was a pouch worn by the diviner who hung it around his loins using the string as a girdle.

The original meaning of *ephod* is "girdle" and the verb *aphad* means "to put on, to gird." David, a strong believer in the Urim and Thummim, danced before the Lord "girded with an ephod," and we must assume that according to the primitive fashion the diviner was otherwise naked. Hence he incurred the contempt of his wife Michal whose piety did not go so far as the king's in worshiping Yahveh in this antiquated manner.

The main significance of the ephod in connection with the Urim and Thummim was to serve as a receptacle for the lots, and so it may very well have become customary to make it of a more costly and enduring material in the form of a vase. This will explain those passages in which the ephod is spoken of as being made of gold and standing on the altar, as where we are informed that the sword of Goliath had been deposited as a trophy wrapped in a mantle "behind the ephod."

There are other passages in which "ephod" seems to be identical with an idol, but if our interpretation be accepted there is no difficulty in this, for the receptacle of the Urim and Thummim may very well have come to be regarded as an object of worship.

It is difficult to say whether the ephod is identical with the *khoshen,* the breastplate of the high priest, which in later postexilic usage was ornamented with twelve precious stones representing the twelve tribes of Israel. It is sure, however, that the Urim and Thummim cannot be identified with the twelve jewels, and the Hebrew words plainly indicate that they were placed inside as into a pouch. In Lev. xiii. 8 the verb *nathan el,* "to put into," is used and not *nathan 'al,* "to put upon."

The breastplate of the high priest seems to be the same as what is called in Babylonian history the "tables of judgment," which also were worn on the breast. But the identification does not seem convincing. We would have to assume that the ephod was first worn around the loins after the fashion of a loin cloth and that later in a more civilised age when the priests were dressed in sacerdotal robes, it was suspended from the shoulders and hung upon the breast.

After Solomon's time there is no longer any historical record of the use of the Urim and Thummim. It seems certain that in the post-exilic age the rabbis knew no more about it than we do to-day and regretted the loss of this special evidence of grace. They supposed their high priests must be no longer fit to consult the oracle (Esdras ii. 63 ; Neh. vii. 65) and Josephus states (*Antiq.* iii. 8-9) that two hundred years before his time, it had ceased. According to common tradition, however, it was never reintroduced into the temple service after the exile.

While Josephus identified the Urim and Thummim with the twelve jewels in the breastplate of the high priest, Philo* claims that they were pictures exhibited in the embroidery of the breastplate representing the symbols of light and truth. His conception is untenable, but it is noteworthy because his view seems to be influenced by his knowledge of the sacerdotal vestments of Egypt. We are told that the high priest in his capacity as judge used to wear a breastplate bearing the image of truth or justice. One such

---

* *De vita Mosis,* p. 670 C; 671, D. E.; *De Monarchia,* p. 824, A.

shield has been found, upon which were two figures recognisable by the emblems on their heads: one with a solar disk as Ra, the sun-god or light, the other with a feather, as Maat or truth. If the Urim and Thummim were not plural and were not contrasts, and if we did not know too well that they were placed in an ephod, Philo's interpretation would have much to recommend itself. Perhaps he and also the Septuagint were under Egyptian influence.

While we do not believe that the Urim and Thummim were exactly like the yang and yin we are fully convinced that the Chinese method of divination throws some light upon the analogous Hebrew practice and will help us to understand the meaning of the terms. If the two systems are historically connected, which is not quite impossible, we must assume that they were differentiated while yet in their most primitive forms.

P'AN-KU.

The basic idea of the yih philosophy was so convincing that it almost obliterated the Taoist cosmogony of P'an-Ku who is said to have chiseled the world out of the rocks of eternity. Though the legend is not held in high honor by the *literati,* it contains some features of interest which have not as yet been pointed out and deserve at least an incidental comment.

P'an-Ku is written in two ways: one[8] means in literal translations, "basin ancient," the other "basin solid."[9] Both are homophones, i. e., they are pronounced the same way; and the former may be preferred as the original and correct spelling. Obviously the name means "aboriginal abyss," or in the terser German, *Urgrund,* and we have reason to believe it to be a translation of the Babylonian *Tiamat,* "the Deep."

The Chinese legend tells us that P'an-Ku's bones changed to rocks; his flesh to earth; his marrow, teeth and nails to metals; his hair to herbs and trees; his veins to rivers; his breath to wind; and his four limbs became pillars marking the four corners of the world, —which is a Chinese version not only of the Norse myth of the Giant Ymir, but also of the Babylonian story of Tiamat.

---

[8] 盤 古   [9] 固

Illustrations of P'an-Ku represent him in the company of supernatural animals that symbolise old age or immortality, viz., the
tortoise and the crane; sometimes also the dragon, the emblem of
power, and the phenix, the emblem of bliss.

*   *   *

When the earth had thus been shaped from the body of P'an-
Ku, we are told that three great rulers successively governed the
world: first the celestial, then the terrestrial, and finally the human
sovereign. They were followed by Yung-Ch'eng and Sui-Jen (i. e.,
fire-man) the latter being the Chinese Prometheus, who brought the
fire down from heaven and taught man its various uses.

The Prometheus myth is not indigenous to Greece, where it
received the artistically classical form under which it is best known
to us. The name, which by an ingenious afterthought is explained
as "the fore thinker," is originally the Sanskrit *pramantha*[10] and
means "twirler" or "fire-stick," being the rod of hard wood which
produced fire by rapid rotation in a piece of soft wood.

We cannot deny that the myth must have been known also in
Mesopotamia, the main center of civilisation between India and
Greece, and it becomes probable that the figure Sui-Jen has been
derived from the same prototype as the Greek Prometheus.

THE FIVE ELEMENTS.

Occultism dominated the development of thought during the
Middle Ages of China not less than in Europe, and here again in
the conception of the elements we find traces of a common origin
in both the East and West.

The Chinese speak of five elements: water, fire, wood, metal,
and earth; while, according to the ancient sages of Hellas and India,
there are but four: water, fire, earth, and air. This latter view also

---

[10] See Steinthal's "The original Form of the Legend of Prometheus"
which forms and appendix to Goldziher's *Mythology Among the Hebrews,*
translated by Russell Martineau, London. 1877.

Mantha is derived from the same root as the German word *mangeln,* "to
torture," and one who forces (viz. Agni, the god of fire) is called *prama-
thyu-s* "the fire-robber." The Sanskrit name in its Greek form is Prometheus,
whose nature of fire-god is still recognisable in the legend.

(although in a later age) has migrated to China, where it is commonly accepted among the Buddhists, but has been modified in so far as ether has been superadded so as to make the elements of the Buddhist-Chinese conception equal in number to the older enumeration which we may call the Taoist view.

CHINESE.   EUROPEAN.   STUPA FORM.   MEMORIAL POLE.

DIFFERENT REPRESENTATIONS OF THE ELEMENTS.

[The proportions of the several heights are deemed important, and are as follows: the square, 10; the circle, 9; the triangle, 7; the crescent, 2; the gem, 6. When built in the form of a *stupa,* the square changes into a cube, the circle into a globe, the triangle into a four-sided pyramid, and the crescent and gem also into solid bodies. The globe retains its proper dimensions but is, as it were, pressed into the cube and the pyramid; the pyramid is frequently changed into an artistically carved roof. The Mediæval European conception is obviously not original.]

That the Buddhist conception of the five elements has been imported to China from India, is proved beyond question by the fact

TIBETAN STUPA.

[This illustration is reproduced from *The East of Asia,* (June 1905), an illustrated magazine printed in Shanghai, China.

The monument represents the five elements, but its shape is no longer exact. The upper part of the cube shows a formation of steps, not unlike the Babylonian zikkurat or staged tower. The globe is no longer a true sphere, and the pyramid has been changed into a pointed cone, so slender as to be almost a pole. The monument is probably used as a mausoleum.]

that the Chinese diagrams are frequently marked with their Sanskrit terms.   It is strange that the symbolic diagrams are more
nearly identical than their interpretations.   Earth is represented
by a square, water by a sphere, fire by a triangle, air by a crescent,

GATEWAY TO BUDDHIST MONASTERY, PEKIN.

A further development of the Stupa of the five elements.

[The cube has been changed into a roofed house; the sphere has
assumed the shape of a Chinese cap, the pyramid is adorned with a
peculiar ornament imitative of a cover, and the crescent has been
changed into a flower-like knob, as has also the gem which surmounts
the whole.]

and ether by a gem surmounting the whole. The two upper symbols
are conceived as one in the treatises of the mediæval alchemy of
Europe, and serve there as the common symbol of air. The symbol
ether is commonly called by its Sanskrit term *mani*, which literally
means "gem," and in popular imagination is endowed with magic
power.

The five elements are also represented by memorial poles which
on the Chinese All Souls' Day are erected at the tombs of the dead,
on which occasion the grave is ornamented with lanterns, and a
torch is lit at evening.

All over the interior of Asia so far as it is dominated by Chinese civilisation, we find *stupas* built in the shape of the symbols
of the five elements, and their meaning is interpreted in the sense
that the body of the dead has been reduced to its original elements.
We must not, however, interpret this idea in a materialistic sense,
for it is meant to denote an absorption into the All and a return
to the origin and source of life.

It is noticeable that this reverence of the elements as divine is
a well-known feature of ancient Mazdaism, the faith of the Persians,
and is frequently alluded to by Herodotus in his description of
Persian customs. The desire not to desecrate the elements causes
the Persians to regard burial and cremation as offensive. They
deposit their dead in the Tower of Silence, leaving them there to
the vultures, whereby the pollution by the corpse either of earth
or of fire is avoided.

The Taoist view of the elements is different from the Buddhist
conception, and we may regard it as originally and typically Chinese. At any rate it is full of occultism and constitutes an important chapter in the mystic lore of China. According to this view,
the five elements are water, fire, wood, metal, and earth.* The knowledge of these elements, legend tells us, is somehow connected with
the marks on the shell of the sacred tortoise which, having risen from
the river Loh, appeared to Ts'ang-Hieh (Mayers, *Ch. R. M.,* I, 756).
Tsou-Yen, a philosopher who lived in the fourth century B. C.,

---

*水 火 木 金 土

wrote a treatise on cosmogony in which the five elements play an important part (Mayers, *Ch. R. M.,* I, 746).

The five elements also figure prominently in "The Great Plan,"[11] which is an ancient imperial manifesto on the art of good government. There it is stated that like everything else they are produced by the yang and yin, being the natural results of that twofold breath which will operate favorably or unfavorably upon the living or the dead according to the combination in which they are mixed. All misfortunes are said to arise from a disturbance of the five elements in a given situation, and thus the Chinese are very careful not to interfere with nature or cause any disturbance of natural conditions. We are told in "The Great Plan"[12] that "in olden times K'wan dammed up the inundating waters and so disarranged the five elements. The Emperor of Heaven was aroused to anger and would not give him the nine divisions of the Great Plan. In this way the several relations of society were disturbed, and [for punishment] he was kept in prison until he died." K'wan's misfortune has remained a warning example to the Chinese. In their anxiety not to disturb the proper mixture in which the five elements should be combined they pay great attention to those pseudo-scientific professors who determine the prevalence of the several elements, not by studying facts but by interpreting some of the most unessential features, for instance, the external shape of rocks and plants. Pointed crags mean "fire"; gently rounded mountains, "metal"; cones and sugar-loaf rocks represent trees, and mean "wood"; and square plateaus denote "earth"; but if the plateau be irregular in shape so as to remind one of the outlines of a lake, it stands for "water." It would lead us too far to enter into further details; at the same time it would be difficult to lay down definite rules, as there is much scope left to the play of the imagination, and it is certain that, while doctors may disagree in the Western world, the geomancers of China have still more opportunity for a great divergence of opinion.

The elements are supposed to conquer one another according

---

[11] A chapter in the *Shu King,* translated into English by James Legge. *S. B. E.,* vol. III, 137.

[12] See *S. B. E.,* III, 139.

to a definite law. We are told that wood conquers earth, earth conquers water, water conquers fire, fire conquers metal, and metal conquers wood. This rule which is preserved by Liu An of the second century B. C. is justified by Pan Ku, a historian of the second century A. D.,compiler of the books of the era of the Han dynasty, as follows:

"By wood can be produced fire, by fire can be produced earth [in other words, wood through fire is changed to ashes]; from earth can be produced metal [i. e., by mining]; from metal can be produced water [they can be changed through heat to a liquid state]; from water can be produced wood [plants]. When fire heats metal, it makes it liquid [i. e., it changes it into

THE FIVE ELEMENTS AND THEIR INTERRELATION.

ELEMENTS	PARENT	CHILD	ENEMY	FRIEND	PLANET
water's	metal	wood	earth	fire	Mercury
fire's	wood	earth	water	metal	Mars
wood's	water	fire	metal	earth	Jupiter
metal's	earth	water	fire	wood	Venus
earth's	fire	metal	wood	water	Saturn

the state of the element water]. When water destroys fire it operates adversely upon the very element by which it is produced. Fire produces earth, yet earth counteracts water. No one can do anything against these phenomena, for the power which causes the five elements to counteract each other is according to the natural dispensation of heaven and earth. Large quantities prevail over small quantities, hence water conquers fire. Spirituality prevails over materiality, the non-substance over substance, thus fire conquers metal; hardness conquers softness, hence metal conquers wood; density is superior to incoherence, therefore, wood conquers earth; solidity conquers insolidity, therefore earth conquers water."

Besides being interrelated as parent and offspring, or as friend and enemy, the five elements are represented by the five planets, so that water corresponds to Mercury, fire to Mars, wood to Jupiter, metal to Venus, and earth to Saturn.

The yih system being cosmic in its nature, has been used by the Chinese sages to represent the universe. The first attempt in this direction is Fuh-Hi's diagram in compass form representing the four quarters and four intermediary directions.

The system was changed by Wen Wang who rearranged the eight trigrams but retained the fundamental idea. It was supposed to have been revealed to Fuh-Hi on the back of a tortoise, but later sages superadded to the fundamental idea further characteristics

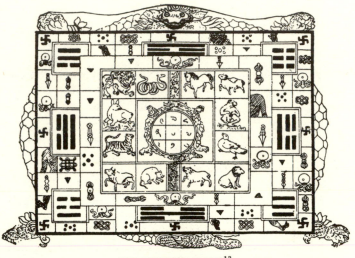

THE MYSTIC TABLET.[13]

of the universe, according to their more complicated knowledge of science and occultism.

We reproduce here a mystic tablet of Tibetan workmanship, which, however, reflects the notions prevailing over the whole Chinese empire. The kwa tablet lies on the back of the tortoise, presumably the same as was supposed to have been present when P'an-Ku chiseled the world from out of the rocks of eternity — and

---

[13] The table has been reproduced from Waddell's *Buddhism of Tibet*, p. 453. Students who take the trouble to enter into further details are warned that in Waddell's table, by some strange mistake, the position of the trigrams *tui* and *chan,* in the east and in the west, has been reversed, a mistake which we have corrected in our reproduction.

certainly the same tortoise which made its appearance in the Loh river to reveal the secret of the kwa to Fuh-Hi.

In the center of our kwa tablet is the magic square written in Tibetan characters, which is the same as that represented in dots in the so-called "Writing of Loh."[14]   It is also depicted as resting in its turn on the carapace of a smaller tortoise.

This magic square is surrounded by the twelve animals of the duodenary cycle, representing both the twelve double-hours of the day, and the twelve months of the year.   In the left lower center is represented the rat which, in passing around to the left, is followed in order by the ox, tiger, hare, dragon, serpent, horse, goat, monkey,

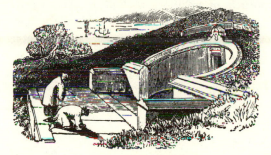

A TYPICAL CHINESE GRAVE.
[The dead are protected against the evil influence of unfavorably mixed elements in the surroundings of the grave by a horseshoe-shaped wall. Cf. pp. 56-57.]

cock, dog, and boar.   The symbols of the days are: a sun for Sunday, a crescent for Monday; a red eye for Tuesday (red light of the planet Mars); a hand holding a coin for Wednesday (indicating the function of the god Mercury); a thunderbolt for Thursday (sacred to Marduk, Jupiter, Thor, the thunder-god); a buckle for Friday (day of Frigga or Venus); and a bundle for Saturday.

The duodenary cycle of animals is surrounded by various emblems indicating lucky and unlucky days.   Among these we can discover gems, buckles, thunderbolts, various limbs of the body, triangles, five-spots, links of a chain, luck symbols, and swastikas.

[14] See the author's pamphlet, *Chinese Philosophy,* p. 19.

They surround the eight trigrams which are placed according to the arrangement of Wen Wang. The kwa in the lower part represents north and winter; in the upper part, the south and summer; toward the right, west and autumn; and toward the left, east and spring. The kwa in the lower right hand corner represents heaven; in the lower left, mountain; the upper left, air or wind; and in the right upper corner, earth.

SYSTEMS OF ENUMERATION.

The twelve animals which are pictured on our Tibetan tablet are a curious relic of prehistoric civilisation. They represent at once the twelve months, the twelve divisions of the zodiac, and the twelve double hours of the day. Kindred systems of designating duodecimal divisions of the cosmos, both in time and space, by a cycle of animals can be traced in Babylon, Egypt, primitive America, and modern Europe, where to the present day the constellations along the ecliptic are divided into twelve groups, called the Zodiac, or *Thierkreis,* i. e., the animal cycle.

The duodenary cycle is an ancient method of counting, expressed by animal names, a custom which has only been abolished in Japan since the Great Reform under the influence of Western civilisation. Up to that time people spoke there of "the rat hour," "the ox hour," "the tiger hour," etc., and these terms had no other significance than in Western countries, one o'clock, two o'clock, or three o'clock.

The twelve animals are affiliated with the twelve branches, so-called, which practically possess the same significance, being also a duodenary cycle. The twelve branches may be summarily characterised as the twelve months, beginning with the eleventh in which the yang principle begins to prepare for its appearance in the new year, and ending in the tenth month of the ensuing year. The twelve branches are correlated not only to the twelve animals, but also to the five elements as indicated in our diagram. The fifth element "earth" is missing because it represents the center around which the twelve branches are grouped.

THE DUODENARY CYCLE.

THE TWELVE BRANCHES

THE TWELVE ANIMALS

NO.	NAME	TRANSCRIPTION	USUAL MEANING	SIGNIFICANCE IN THE DUODENARY CYCLE	SYMBOL	ELEMENT TO WHICH RELATED	NAME	MEANING
1	子	tze	child	Regeneration of vegetation	Yang stirring underground	water	鼠	rat
2	丑	chu	cord	Relaxation; untying a knot	Hand half-opened	water	牛	ox
3	寅	yin	to revere	Awakening of life	Wriggling earthworm	wood	虎	tiger
4	卯	mao	a period of time	Plants breaking through the soil	Opening a gate	wood	兔	hare
5	辰	chen	vibration	First vegetation; seed-time	Thunderstorm	wood	龍	dragon
6	巳	ssu	end	Supremacy of Yang	Snake	fire	蛇	serpent
7	午	wu	to oppose	Yin reasserting itself	Female principle in hidden growth	fire	馬	horse
8	未	wei	not yet	Taste of fruit	Tree in full bloom	fire	羊	goat
9	申	shen	to expand	Yin growing strong	Clasped hands	metal	猴	monkey
10	酉	yu	ripe	Completion	Cider or wine-press	metal	雞	cock
11	戌	shu	guard	Exhaustion	Yang withdrawing underground	metal	犬	dog
12	亥	hai	[Kernel]*	Kernel or root	Yang in touch with Yin	water	猪	boar

* This character has now no meaning except in its relation to the duodenary cycle. Formerly it denoted kernel, but now the character for tree is added to give that meaning.

There is another system of counting, which however is decimal, and is called "the ten stems"; and it appears that it is simply an older method of counting the months of the year. In their original here also the explanation of the several symbols has reference to the progress of the year.

It is not impossible that the decimal system was the original and indigenous Chinese method of counting, while the duodecimal system

THE TEN STEMS.

NO.	NAME	TRANSCRIPTION	SIGNIFICANCE	ELEMENT TO WHICH RELATED	
1	甲	chia	Yang moving in the East sprouting.	fir tree	} wood
2	乙	yi	Plant growing in a crooked way; tendril; twig.	bamboo	
3	丙	ping	Growth in southern heat; bloom.	torch-flame	} fire
4	丁	ting	Vegetation in warm season; summer.	lamp-light	
5	戊	wu	Exuberance; surcease of life.	mountains	} earth
6	己	ki	Wintry sleep; hibernation.	level ground	
7	庚	keng	Fullness of crops; the West; autumn fruit.	weapon	} metal
8	辛	sin	Ripened fruit and its flavor; supposed to be metallic.	cauldron	
9	壬	jen	Yin at the height of its function; pregnancy.	billow	} water
10	癸	kwei	Water absorbed by earth; Yang preparing for spring.	unruffled stream	

was imported at a very early date from Accad or Sumer, the country of the founders of Babylonian civilisation.

The existence of these two systems suggests the occurrence of a calendar reform such as was introduced in Rome under Numa Pompilius, and we are confronted with the strange coincidence that in China as well as in Rome the two additional months (January and February) were inserted at the beginning as a result of which we call even to-day the last month of the year December, i. e., "the tenth." We must leave the question as to the plausibility of a historical connection to specialists familiar with the influence of Babylonian thought on the rest of the world. It is not impossible that a Babylonian (perhaps Sumerian) calendar reform traveled in both directions, rapidly toward the more civilised East, and very slowly toward the West, producing in these remote countries and at different times this startling coincidence of a similar calendar reform.

We might parenthetically state that the original meaning of the ten stems and twelve branches has practically been lost sight of, and both systems have become simply series of figures, the former from one to ten, the latter from one to twelve; while their symbolical relations, the former with the elements, the latter with the twelve animals, are of importance merely to occultists.

The ten stems are also called "the ten mothers," and the twelve branches, "the twelve children." That the former is the older arrangement appears from another name which is "the ten hoary characters.

By a combination of the ten stems with the twelve branches in groups of two in which the former are repeated six times and the latter five times, a series of sixty is produced which is commonly called by sinologists the sexagenary cycle, and is used for naming years as well as days. The invention of the sexagenary cycle and its application to the calendar is attributed to Nao the Great, one of the prime ministers of Hwang Ti, the Yellow Emperor,[15] who had solicited this work in the sixtieth year of his reign. Nao the Great, having accomplished the task, set the beginning of the new era in the succeeding year, 2637 B. C. Accordingly we live now in the seventy-sixth cycle which began in 1863 and will end in 1922.

A convenient method of translating the properly Chinese names of the sexagenary cycle would be to render the two characters by their equivalent relations to the twelve animals and the five elements,

---

[15] According to traditional chronology, Hwang Ti reigned from 2697 to 2597 B. C.

THE SEXAGENARY CYCLE.

甲	子	1 chia tzu 1864	甲	申	21 chia shên 1884	甲	辰	41 chia chên 1904
乙	丑	2 yi ch'ou 1865	乙	酉	22 yi yu 1885	乙	巳	42 yi ssu 1905
丙	寅	3 ping yin 1866	丙	戌	23 ping shu 1886	丙	午	43 ping wu 1906
丁	卯	4 ting mao 1867	丁	亥	24 ting hai 1887	丁	未	44 ting wei 1907
戊	辰	5 mou chên 1868	戊	子	25 mou tzu 1888	戊	申	45 mou shên 1908
巳	巳	6 chi ssu 1869	己	丑	26 chi ch'ou 1889	巳	酉	46 chi yu 1909
庚	午	7 kêng wu 1870	庚	寅	27 kêng yin 1890	庚	戌	47 kêng shu 1910
辛	未	8 hsin wei 1871	辛	卯	28 hsin mao 1891	辛	亥	48 hsin hai 1911
壬	申	9 jên shen 1872	壬	辰	29 jên shên 1892	壬	子	49 jên tzu 1912
癸	酉	10 kwei yu 1873	癸	巳	30 kwei ssu 1893	癸	丑	50 kwei ch'ou 1913
甲	戌	11 chia shu 1874	甲	午	31 chia wu 1894	甲	寅	51 chia yin 1914
乙	亥	12 yi hai 1875	乙	未	32 yi wei 1895	乙	卯	52 yi mao 1915
丙	子	13 ping tzu 1876	丙	申	33 ping shên 1896	丙	辰	53 ping chên 1916
丁	丑	14 ting ch'ou 1877	丁	酉	34 ting yu 1897	丁	巳	54 ting ssu 1917
戊	寅	15 mou yin 1878	戊	戌	35 mou shu 1898	戊	午	55 mou wu 1918
巳	卯	16 chi mao 1879	己	亥	36 chi hai 1899	巳	未	56 chi wei 1919
庚	辰	17 kêng chên 1880	庚	子	37 kêng tzu 1900	庚	申	57 kêng shên 1920
辛	巳	18 hsin ssu 1881	辛	丑	38 hsin ch'ou 1901	辛	酉	58 hsin wu 1921
壬	午	19 jên wu 1882	壬	寅	39 jên yin 1902	壬	戌	59 jên shu 1922
癸	未	20 kwei wei 1883	癸	卯	40 kwei mao 1903	癸	亥	60 kwei hai 1923

so as to speak of the "fir-rat" year, the "bamboo-ox" year, the "torch-tiger" year, etc.

FENG-SHUI.*

Chinese occultism has been reduced to a system in an occult science (or better, pseudo-science) called *feng-shui* which, literally translated, means "wind and water," and the two words combined denote atmospheric influence, or climate. As a science feng-shui means a study of conditions, spiritual as well as physical, and the average Chinese is very anxious to locate the site of graves, temples, public and private edifices so as to insure the auspicious influence of their surroundings. Belief in the efficiency of feng-shui is very strong, and consequently its scholars play an important part in public and private life.

The science of feng-shui is fantastical, but its advocates claim the authority of the ancient *Yih King,* which in chapter XIII, 1 to 12, reads as follows:

"By looking up in order to contemplate the heavenly bodies, and by looking down to examine into the natural influences of the earth, man may acquire a knowledge of the cause of darkness and light."

Feng-shui is also called *ti-li*† and *k'an-yü*.‡ *Ti-li* may fitly be translated by "geomancy." *Li,* frequently translated by "reason" or "rational principle," means a system of the dominant maxims which govern nature. *Ti* means "the earth" and so the two together signify "the divining art as to terrestrial conditions." *K'an-yü,* translated literally, means "canopy chariot," but *k'an* (canopy) refers to the sky and *yü* (chariot) refers to the earth as the vehicle in which all living beings are carried. The term "canopy chariot" then means the art which is occupied with the conditions of man's habitation.

The professional diviners who practise *feng-shui* are called *sien-sheng,*§ "the elder born," which is a title of respect and has been translated by "professor." They are called either *feng-shui sien-sheng,* "professors of divination," or *ti-li sien-sheng,* "geomancers," or *k'an-yü sien-sheng,* "masters of the canopied chariot."

---

*風水　　†地理　　‡堪輿　　§先生

The application of the feng-shui is naturally very loose, and two different professors may easily come to opposite results according to their individual interpretation of the correct balance of the mixture of the elements and the several spiritual influences that may be discovered in special localities. Diviners use for their geomantic investigations a peculiar instrument with a mariner's compass in the center the purpose of which De Groot explains as follows:

"The chief use of the geomantic compass is to find the line in which, according to the almanac, a grave ought to be made, or a house or temple built. Indeed, in this most useful of all books it is every year decided between which two points of the compass the lucky line for that year lies, and which point is absolutely inauspicious. This circumstance not only entails a postponement of many burials, seeing it is not always possible to find a grave, answering to all the geomantic requirements, in the lucky line of the year; but it regularly compels the owners of houses and temples to postpone repairs or the rebuilding of the same until a year in which the line wherein their properties are situate is declared to be lucky. Many buildings for this reason alone are allowed to fall to ruin for years, and it is no rare thing to see whole streets simultaneously demolished and rebuilt in years auspicious to the direction in which they were placed."

Considering the sacrifices which are expected of a good son in the selection of the site and the general equipment of the parental graves, we can easily understand that the burden of ancestral worship is very heavy. While we must admire the filial piety of the Chinese, we regret to see the uselessness of their devotion and the waste to which it leads. It is refreshing, however, to observe that the general rule is not without exceptions and we find that there are sensible men who raise their voices in protest.

Ts'ui Yuen of the second century, a mandarin of high position, died at Loh-Yang, the imperial metropolis. According to the customary ritual, his son should have transported his remains to his place of birth for burial in the family cemetery, but Ts'ui Yuen left these instructions with his son Shih, which we quote from De Groot (*loc. cit.,* pp. 837-8):

---

[16] In his voluminous work *The Religious System of China,* Vol. III, Bk. 1. "Disposal of the Dead." Part 3. "The Grave," p. 974.

"Human beings borrow from heaven and earth the breath upon which they live, and at the end of their terrestrial career they restitute the etherial parts of that breath to heaven, giving their bones back to earth; consequently, what part of the earth can be unsuitable for concealing their skeletons? You must not take me back to my place of birth, nor may you accept any funeral presents, neither offerings of mutton or pork."

The Chinese authority from which Professor De Groot quotes, adds:[17]

"Respectfully receiving these his last orders, Shih kept the corpse in Loh-Yang and there buried it."

The spirit of Ts'ui Yuen has not died out, as is attested by a satirical poem which is current to-day, and which humorously points out the inconsistency of those mantics or soothsayers who know all the conditions of the four quarters and promise their patrons to show them (for a due consideration) a spot so auspicious for a grave that the spirit of their ancestor will bestow upon members of the family the dignity of kings. If that were true, why have they not buried their own parents there? The poem in the original Chinese is as follows:

地理先生慣説謊、
指南指北指西東、
山中若有王侯地、
何不尋來葬乃翁.

ti li hsien sheng kwan shuo huang
chih nan chih pei chih hsi tung
shan chung je yu wang hou ti
he pu hsin lai tsang nai weng.[18]

This translation imitates the original as closely as possible in metre and meaning:

Trash these mantics manifest,
Point out south, north, east and west;
Know graves royalty bestowing
Yet their own sires there not rest.

[17] *Books of the Later Han Dynasty,* Chap. 82 line 15.

[18] In the early Chinese form, the final words of the first, second, and fourth lines were all pronounced as if ending in *ong*. Consequently, although the individual words have changed their form, the series is considered as containing one rhyme and, according to Chinese rules of rhyming, is still so used in verse.

LO-PAN.

Collectors of curios may have seen in Chinese stores the instrument called *lo-pan** (net-tablet), or *lo-king*† (net-standard), or *pan-
shih*‡ (disk-norm). This is the geomancer's compass which incorpo-

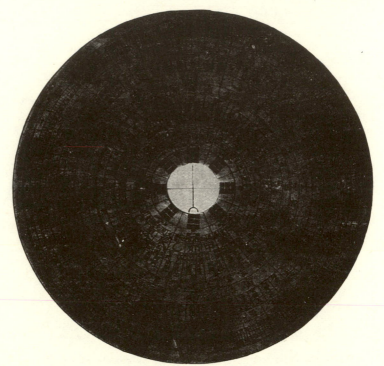

LO-PAN OR NET TABLET.
[The original is in the possession of Prof. Friedrich Hirth.]

rates the sum-total of feng-shui. The Chinese salesman who showed
the instrument at my request, a man who must have lived half his
life or more in the United States, expressed great respect for it
and tried to impress me with the fact that it contained the deepest
wisdom of the ages.

The lo-pan is a disk of lacquered wood, mostly of yellow color,

---

* 羅盤   † 羅經   ‡ 盤式

carrying in its center under glass, a small mariner's compass. Some of the characters written in the surrounding circles are red, and some are black. Different copies differ in details, but all are practically the same in their general and most characteristic features. The concentric circles of the net tablet are called *ts'eng*,* i. e., "tiers," "stories," or "strata."

The mariner's compass in the center represents *t'ai chih*,† "the great origin." The first circle contains the eight trigrams in the arrangement of Fuh-Hi, which denote the eight directions of the compass and the virtues and properties attributed to them.

The second circle contains the numerals from one to nine in the arrangement of the magic square, the five being omitted as it belongs in the center. Accordingly the sum of each two opposite figures always makes ten.

The third row represents twenty-four celestial constellations, each expressed in two characters, so that three names are registered in each octant.

The fourth circle represents in occult terms twenty-four divisions of the compass. Southeast, southwest, northeast, and northwest are written in their kwa names, while the rest are designated alternately by the ten stems and twelve branches; two of the stems are omitted, however, because referring to the element earth, they are supposed to belong in the center. If we write the ten stems as numerals from one to ten, the twelve branches in italic letters from *a* to *m*, and the four kwa names in Roman capitals A to D, we have the following arrangement, beginning in the southeast: A *f* 3 *g* 4 *h* B *i* 7 *k* 8 *l* C *m* 9 *a* 10 *b* D *c* 1 *d* 2 *e*. This arrangement is ancient for it is quoted as an established part of the divining method by Sze-Ma Ch'ien in the twenty-fifth chapter of his *Historical Records,* which is devoted to the art of divination.

The fifth circle is divided into seventy-two parts each containing two characters of the sexagenary cycle, written one above the other, and arranged in groups of five divided by blank spaces. If we again express the ten stems in figures and the twelve branches

---

in italics, the scheme (starting with the first branch *a* standing in the north) reads as follows:

1 3 5 7 9	2 4 6 8 10	3 5 7 9 1	4 6 8 10 2	5 7 9 1 3	6 8 10 2 4
a a a a a	*b b b b b*	*c c c c c*	*d d d d d*	*e e e e e*	*f f f f f*

7 9 1 3 5	8 10 2 4 6	9 1 3 5 7	10 2 4 6 8	1 3 5 7 9	2 4 6 8 10
g g g g g	*h h h h h*	*i i i i*	*k k k k k*	*l l l l l*	*m m m m m*

In the sixth row each octant is divided into three sections, each having five compartments in the second and fourth of which appear two characters of the sexagenary cycle. Accordingly they are arranged in the following order, the blanks being expressed by zeros:

0 3 0 7 0	0 3 0 7 0	0 4 0 8 0	0 4 0 8 0	0 3 0 7 0	0 3 0 7 0
0 *a* 0 *a* 0	0 *a* 0 *a* 0	0 *b* 0 *b* 0	0 *b* 0 *b* 0	0 *c* 0 *c* 0	0 *c* 0 *c* 0

0 4 0 8 0	0 4 0 8 0	0 3 0 7 0	0 3 0 7 0	0 4 0 8 0	0 4 0 8 0
0 *d* 0 *d* 0	0 *d* 0 *d* 0	0 *e* 0 *e* 0	0 *e* 0 *e* 0	0 *f* 0 *f* 0	0 *f* 0 *f* 0

0 3 0 7 0	0 3 0 7 0	0 4 0 8 0	0 4 0 8 0	0 3 0 7 0	0 3 0 7 0
0 *g* 0 *g* 0	0 *g* 0 *g* 0	0 *h* 0 *h* 0	0 *h* 0 *h* 0	0 *i* 0 *i* 0	0 *i* 0 *i* 0

0 4 0 8 0	0 4 0 8 0	0 3 0 7 0	0 3 0 7 0	0 4 0 8 0	0 4 0 8 0
0 *k* 0 *k* 0	0 *k* 0 *k* 0	0 *l* 0 *l* 0	0 *l* 0 *l* 0	0 *m* 0 *m* 0	0 *m* 0 *m* 0

The third and fourth stems refer to fire and the seventh and eighth to metal.

The seventh row is devoted to the eight stars of the Dipper, which in Chinese folklore is regarded with much awe, because this most conspicuous constellation revolves around the polar star and seems to resemble the hand of a watch on the great celestial dial of the universe. We must remember that the seventh star is double, its luminous satellite being visible even without the assistance of a telescope. If we represent the names of the eight stars by numbers from one to eight, their arrangement beginning with the southwest is as follows: 1 8 5 7 4 4 6 2 3 1 5 7 8 1 3 2 6 6 4 7 5 8 3 2.

Beyond the seventh circle we have a double line which divides the seven inner rows from the nine outer ones. The first of these, the eighth circle, is divided into twelve sections each having three characters, the central ones written in red being the sun and moon together with the five elements twice repeated. Beginning in the south with the character sun, and turning toward the left, they read as follows: sun, moon, water, metal, fire, wood, earth, earth, wood, fire, metal, water.

The ninth row, consisting of twelve sections, represents the twelve branches in regular succession, beginning in the north with the first and turning toward the right. They coincide in position with the twelve branches as they appear in the fourth row.

The tenth row is a repetition of the fifth, with the exception that here the characters are distributed evenly over the whole circle.

The eleventh row consists of numerals only. The circle is divided into twelve sections, each being subdivided into five compartments which contain the following scheme repeated twelve times: | 3 7 | 1 | 5 | 1 | 7 3 |.

The twelfth row is inscribed with the names of the sub-divisions of the four seasons, beginning with early spring above the unalloyed yin and turning toward the right.

SPRING.

立 春 Beginning of Spring.
雨 水 Rain Water.
驚 蟄 Resurrection of hibernating Insects.
春 分 Vernal Equinox.
清 明 Pure Brightness.
穀 雨 Rains over the Grain.

AUTUMN.

立 秋 Beginning of Autumn.
處 暑 Limit of Heat.
白 露 White Dew.
秋 分 Autumnal Equinox.
寒 露 Cold Dew.
霜 降 Descent of Hoar Frost.

SUMMER.

立 夏 Beginning of Summer.
小 滿 Grain filling a little.
芒 種 Grain in Ear.
夏 至 Summer Solstice.
小 暑 Slight Heat.
大 暑 Great Heat.

WINTER.

立 冬 Beginning of Winter.
小 雪 Little Snow.
大 雪 Heavy Snow.
冬 至 Winter Solstice.
小 寒 Little Cold.
大 寒 Severe Cold.

The thirteenth row is divided into seventy-two equal parts, which are left blank.

The fifteenth row is divided into three hundred and sixty equal blanks representing the degrees of a circle which method of division the Chinese as well as we of the Occident have inherited from the Babylonians.

The sixteenth row contains the names of the twenty-eight constellations together with the number of degrees which each covers. These degrees are specifically marked in the fourteenth circle in which the odd numbers only are expressed. The series starting in the southeast and turning toward the right, is as follows:

1. The horn, 11°; in Virgo.
2. The neck, 11°; in Virgo.
3. The bottom, 18°; in Libra.
4. The room, 5°; in Scorpio.
5. The heart, 8°; in Scorpio.
6. The tail, 15°; in Scorpio.
7. The sieve, 9°; in Sagittarius.
8. The measure, 24°; in Sagittarius.
9. The ox, 8°; in Aries and Sagittarius.
10. The damsel, 11°; in Aquarius.
11. The void, 10°; in Aquarius and Equuleus.
12. Danger, 20°; in Aquarius and Pegasus.
13. The house, 16°; in Pegasus.
14. The wall, 13°; in Pegasus and Andromeda.
15. Astride, 11°; in Andromeda and Pisces.
16. The hump, 13°; in Aries.
17. The stomach, 12°; in Musca Borealis.
18. The Pleiades, 9°. (In Chinese *mao*.)[19]
19. The end, 15°; in Hyades and Taurus.
20. The bill or beak, 1°; in Orion.
21. Crossing, or mixture, 11°; in Orion.
22. The well or pond, 31°; in Gemini.
23. The ghost, 5°; in Cancer.
24. The willow, 17°; in Hydra.

---

[19] The Chinese term *mao* does not possess any other significance except the name of this constellation. This character is unfortunately misprinted in Mayers, *Chinese Reader's Manual*. It is correct in the enumeration of Professor De Groot, *loc. cit.,* p. 972.

25. The star, 8°; in Hydra.
26. The drawn bow, 18°; in Hydra.
27. The wing, 17°; in Crater and Hydra.
28. The back of a carriage seat, 13°; in Corvus.

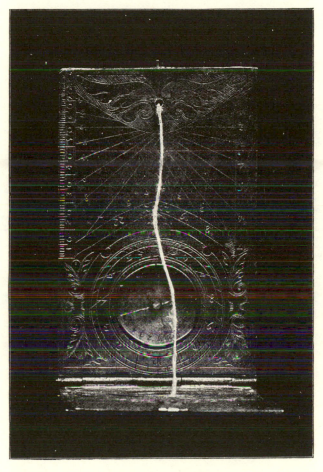

EUROPEAN COMPASS.
(Presumably Italian.)

The two plates are hinged together and fold upon one another in
the same way as the European compasses shown in the following
pages.

THE MARINER'S COMPASS A CHINESE INVENTION.

The lo-pan or net tablet unquestionably serves superstitious purposes, but we must bear in mind that much genuine science is incorporated in many of its details, and the latter no doubt has given
countenance to the former. This again is according to the general
law of the evolution of mankind and finds its parallel in the history
of European civilisation. We must bear in mind that the great
occultists of the Middle Ages, Paracelsus. Albertus Magnus, and

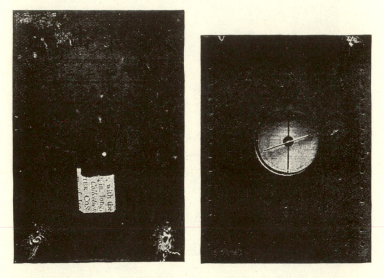

CHINESE POCKET COMPASS.

men like them down to Agrippa of Nettesheim, were the most
powerful intellects of their day; and thougfi they were deeply en-
tangled in mysticism, much of their life's work was devoted to the
furtherance of genuine scientific enquiry.

In the Chinese Middle Ages the leading thinkers were of the
same stamp, and so it is natural that much of genuine astronomy
and the results of accurate observation of the stars are incorporated
in the lo-pan. The most obvious part of it which must have ap-

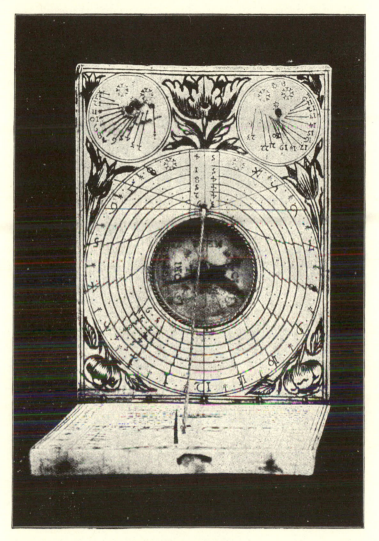

EUROPEAN COMPASS.
(Presumably Nuremberg.)

peared extremely mystifying in former centuries was, as the Chinese call it, the south-pointing needle—the mariner's compass—situated in the center of the lo-pan.

The south-pointing needle is an ancient Chinese invention which for some time seems to have been forgotten. Professor Friedrich Hirth of Columbia University has privately communicated to me facts which prove that it was employed in ancient times by travelers through the desert, that the invention was lost and had to be rediscovered. We would add, too, that the Chinese invention became known in Europe after the time of Marco Polo where it was soon used as a mariner's compass. The incident is well known and can easily be established on the testimony of literary sources, but while sauntering through the National Museum at Washington, the writer discovered a palpable evidence in the show cases there exhibited, which displayed the Chinese pocket instruments containing south-pointing needles presumably a few centuries old, side by side with European compasses. They are of the same oblong shape and consist of two tablets hinged in the same manner. The European instruments have sun-dials in addition and are decidedly more serviceable for practical use but we can not doubt that for the original idea our ancestors are indebted to our Mongol fellow-men.*

THE PERSONIFICATION OF STARS.

To the Chinese (as also in some respects to the Babylonians) the stars are actual presences who sway the destinies of mankind, and we reproduce here a series of illustrations from a Buddhist picture-book printed in Japan. They are based upon ancient traditions ultimately derived from Sumer and Accad, but we have at present no means to determine the question of their history, especially as to their fate in China. One thing, however, may be regarded as certain, viz., that their traditional forms are prior to the calendar reform of the Jesuits. Hence we must assume that they have been imported by the way on

---

* We wish to express here our indebtedness to the National Museum and its officers, and especially to Prof. Otis T. Mason and Mr. George C. Maynard. for the reproduction of characteristic specimens of this interesting collection.

land either by the Buddhists from India, or through some earlier
civilising influences perhaps from ancient Babylon, or may be in
later times from Greece by way of Bactria and Tibet. An historical

諸天

貪狼星 第一	北斗	日輪
樞 璇 璣 權 玉衡 開陽 搖光破軍菩薩 日輪菩薩	大星宮定 周七百廿里中星四 百八十里小星百廿里 論語曰 天文志曰北極	名義藕剥那此云日輪 實德菩薩 造天地經云佛念 遮天地經云佛念 白虎通云 日徑千里周三千 里下於天七千里
巨文星 第二	明星	月輪
月輪菩薩	明星八月八日隱レ日末顯日役中間二 出ル明閉不二迷悟二如 全無ナリ サレバテ 守合三卜 ダル故明星ノ二字ニ三光ヲ備ハ、ナリ	名義集云藕 摩此云 月神造 天地經 云佛念 吉祥菩薩 薩造月

connection of some kind or other with Western astronomy which
also derives its origin from ancient Babylon, can scarcely be doubted;
for the general similarities are too pronounced, and the more par-

ticular ones serve as obvious evidences which cannot be rejected, while the differences afford suggestions in regard to their development and fate.

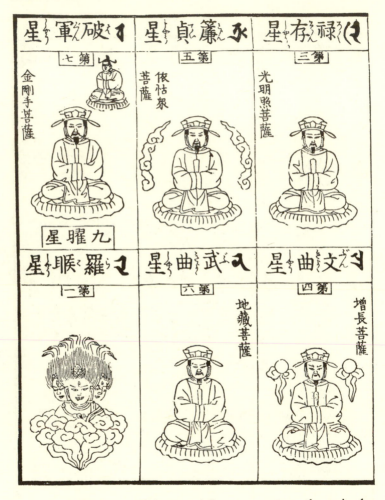

According to the Chinese and Japanese custom, the series begins in the right upper corners and the order proceeds downwards and to the left.

The first figure represents the sun; the second, the moon. In

the next row we see the polar star seated (like Buddha) on a lotus
and holding in his hands a wheel to indicate that he is the hub of
the heavens. As Buddha in the spiritual world, so the polar star

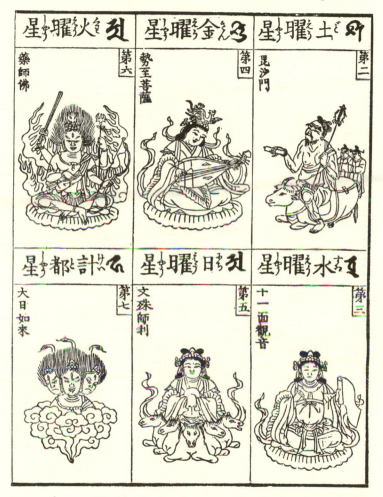

among the constellations is alone at rest while all other things in the
universe whirl round in unceasing rotation. In the same column is
the star of twilight-brightness, which may be either the morning or
evening star.

The third row of the same page begins the series of stars that constitute Ursa Major, popularly called "the dipper" in America and known in China as "the bushel."

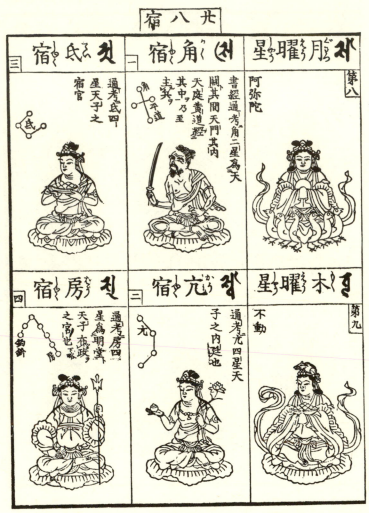

The satellite of the seventh star in Ursa Major is pictured as a smaller companion in the right hand corner in the field of his bigger brother. Since he stands at the very point of the constellation, his significance is in inverse proportion to his size, in a similar way as Tom Thumb always takes the initiative in all deeds and proves to be the saviour of his seven brothers.

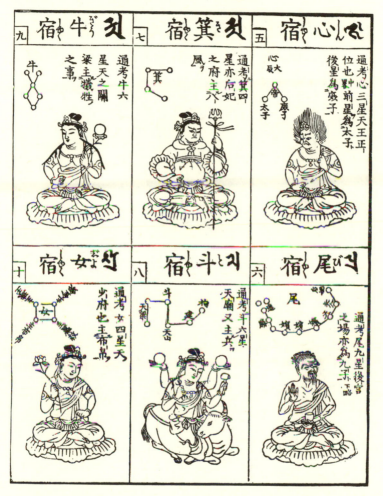

The seven stars of Ursa Major are very conspicuous in the northern firmament, and turn around in the sky like a big hand on the celestial dial pointing out the hour in the clock work of the universe. There is a proverbial saying in China which incorporates the popular Chinese view as follows:

"When the handle of the northern bushel (*Peh Tao*) points

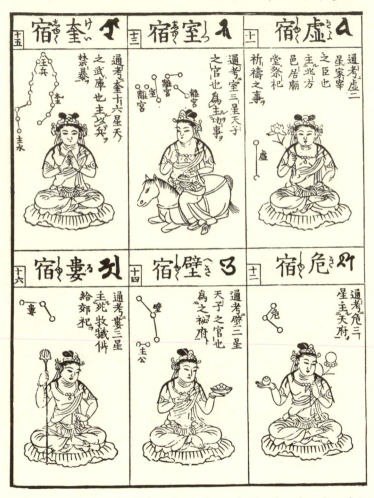

east at nightfall it is spring throughout the land; when it points south, it is summer; when west, it is autumn; and when north, winter."

The three stars ι, κ, λ of Ursa Major are supposed to be the residence of the three councilor spirits mentioned in the *Kan Ying P'ien* as recording the deeds of men, and thus our constellation is symbolically identified in the imagination of the Chinese, with divine justice.

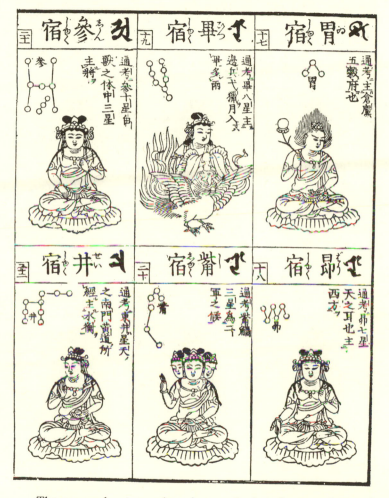

The seven planets are here increased after the precedence of Hindu astrology by two three-headed figures called *Rahu* and *Ketu,* the former being conceived as the head, and the latter as the tail of the dragon who is supposed to be responsible for solar and lunar eclipses. Rahu represents the ascending and Ketu the descending nodes in the ecliptic.

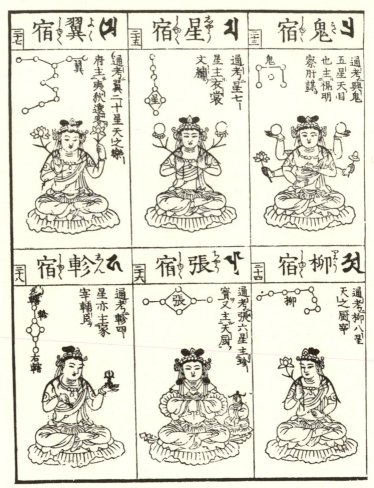

The nine personalities which correspond to the seven planets plus Rahu and Ketu are in Hindu mythology called: Surya, the Sun; Chandra, the moon; Mangala, Mars; Buddha, Mercury; Vrihaspati, Jupiter; Sukra, Venus; Sani, Saturn; while Ketu and Rahu

are identified with stars in the Dragon. Rahu is represented head-
less and Ketu as a trunkless head. A representation of this Hindu
notion is found in Colonel Stuart's zodiac picture reproduced in
Moor's *Hindu Pantheon,* Plate XLVIII. It shows Surya the sun
in the center drawn by seven horses, with Aruna as charioteer. Surya
in the colored original is in gold, while Aruna is painted deep red.
Chandra rides an antelope, Mangala a ram, Buddha is seated on a

A HINDU ZODIAC.

carpet; Rahu and Ketu here interrupt the regular order, the former
being represented as riding on an owl, while the latter, a mere head,
is placed on a divan. Vrihaspati like Buddha is seated on an animal
that may have been intended for a cat, while Sani rides on a raven.

Next in order on our tables beginning with the second column

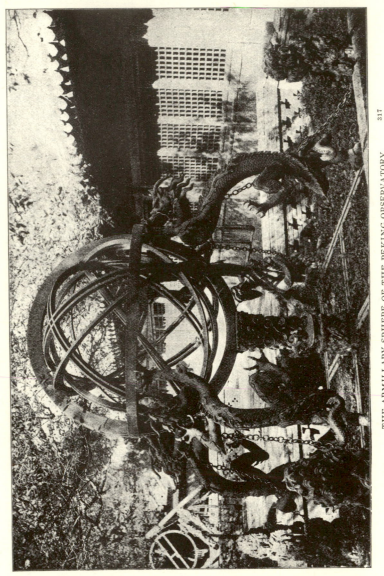

THE ARMILLARY SPHERE OF THE PEKING OBSERVATORY.

317

of their fourth page, are the twenty-eight constellations mentioned above which play an important part in Chinese occultism. The approximate outline of the constellation is indicated in each case above the picture, and we see, for instance, why the fifteenth constellation is called "astride," and the twenty-sixth, a "drawn bow."

We add here to our illustrations of stars a picture of Chih Nü and Keng Niu, the stars Vega and Aquila on either side of the Milky Way, of which Chinese folklore tells one of the prettiest fairy-tales of China. It is briefly thus: The sun-god had a daughter Chih Nü (star Vega = α in Lyre) who excelled by her skill in weaving and her industrial habits. To recompense her he had her

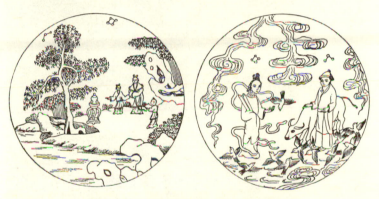

THE SPINNING DAMSEL AND COWHERD.

A Chinese fairy tale of the star Vega. A native illustration from
Williams's *Middle Kingdom.*

married to Keng Niu the herdsman (constellation Aquila), who herded his cattle on the silver stream of heaven (the Milky Way). As soon as married, Chih Nü changed her habits for the worse; she forsook her loom and gave herself up to merry-making and idleness. Thereupon her father decided to separate the lovers by the stream and placed them each on one side of the Milky Way, allowing the husband to meet his wife over a bridge of many thousand mag-pies only once a year, on the seventh day of the seventh month, which is a holy day in China even now.

We know that the Chinese government has kept an impe-

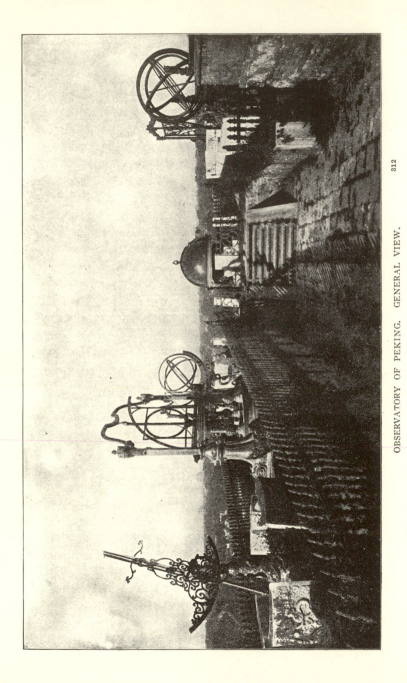

OBSERVATORY OF PEKING. GENERAL VIEW.

rial astronomer since prehistoric times, for the office is mentioned
in the earliest documents. The famous emperor Kang Hi erected

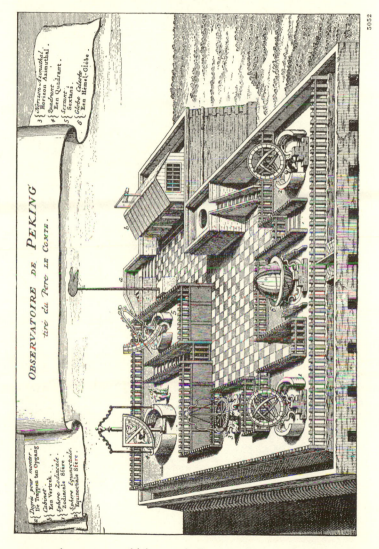

a new observatory which was built according to the instructions
of the Jesuit fathers whose learning at that time was highly re-

SPHERICAL ASTROLABE OF THE PEKING OBSERVATORY.

319

spected in China. The instruments remained at Peking until the Boxer riots when they were removed to Germany at the command of Emperor William.

Our illustrations will enable the reader to form a clear conception of the instruments as well as the style in which they have been put up. They stand on a high platform overlooking the city, surrounded by battlements in the style of an old fortress. One general view is a reproduction of an old cut at the time of the erection of the observatory under the Jesuit fathers. The other one is a photograph made in modern times and showing the instruments *in situ* before their removal to Potsdam.

The gem of the collection is decidedly the spherical astrolabe which has been made after the instructions of Ko Chow King, astronomer royal of emperor Tai Tsu, of the Yüan dynasty, the founder of Peking. It is said to be a marvel of Chinese art. In the general view we notice a quadrant on the left-hand side between two light columns in French style. It is a present of King Louis XIV sent to the emperor Kang Hi in the seventeenth century. Among the instruments preserved in the shed there are some curios of great artistic and historical value. The whole observatory as it stood has always been regarded as one of the most noteworthy treasures of the Tartar capital of the Celestial Empire.

PREHISTORIC CONNECTIONS.

The evidences that indicate a Western origin of Chinese civilisation are very strong, and it seems that the first Chinese settlers must have come in prehistoric times from a country that was closely connected with the founders of Babylonian culture. There is an unmistakable resemblance between cuneiform writing and Chinese script, so as to make it quite probable that they have been derived from a common source. We have, further, the sexagenary cycle corresponding to the use of the number sixty in Babylonia, and many similarities in astronomical names and notions. Moreover, the Chinese divide the circle into three hundred and sixty degrees as did the Babylonians, a system which has been adhered to in the West down to modern times.

GREAT CELESTIAL GLOBE OF THE PEKING OBSERVATORY.

The Prometheus legend seems to come from the same source (presumably Akkad) as the story of the Chinese "Fire Man," Sui-Jen. The Babylonian story of Tiamat as to the formation of the world is repeated in the legend of P'an-Ku, the personification of the ancient abyss.

Finally the yih system of the yang and the yin is paralleled in at least one Semitic tribe by the similar divining method of the Urim and Thummim. Though in the latter case the loss of details prevents us from having any evidence of a historical connection, the similarity of the purpose, as well as the duality of the elements of the oracle cannot be denied.

If none of these indications is conclusive when considered separately, we can not disregard them when all are taken together.

Further bearing in mind that there is an ancient tradition in China of a settlement having been made by a tribe coming from the Far West, we may very well assume the ancestors of the Chinese to be a detachment of the founders of the Babylonian civilisation, either Sumerians or Akkadians, and that they left their home in prehistoric times presumably even before the first Semitic invasion or soon afterwards. They were perhaps that portion of the people who would not submit to the new condition of things and preferred exile to absorption by a victorious enemy.

Our proposition that even in prehistoric times a connection must have existed between all civilised nations of the East and of the West, will be further borne out by the additional evidence furnished by a comparative study of the several calendar systems, as based upon the sun's course through the zodiac, and it is remarkable that it includes even the Mayas of Central America. Since the subject is interesting but rather complicated, requiring considerable space and the reproduction of many illustrations, we shall discuss it in a special chapter,

ZODIACS OF DIFFERENT NATIONS.

WITH REFERENCE TO CHINA.

HOW close must have been the interrelation of primitive mankind, how keen their observation of nature, and considering
their limitations when compared with modern methods, how pro-
found after all, their philosophy, their science, their astronomy,
their physics, their mechanics! In spite of the absence of railroads,
steamers, postal service and telegraph, there must have been a
communication of thought which is as yet little appreciated. Ideas,
the interpretation of nature, and the conception of things divine
as well as secular, must have traveled from place to place. Their
march must have been extremely slow, but they must have gone
out and spread from nation to nation. They had to cross seas and
deserts. They had to be translated into new tongues, but they
traveled in spite of all obstacles. This is certain because we find
among the most remote nations of the earth kindred notions the
similarity of which can scarcely be explained as a mere parallelism.

I will say here that I arrived at the theory of an interconnection
of primitive mankind not because I sought it, but because I tried
to collect unequivocal instances to the contrary, and so I naturally
deem it a well-assured conclusion.

The human mind will naturally pass through certain phases of
evolution and man will necessarily, and in different places in perfect
independence develop certain definite ideas of ghosts, of gods, of
devils, of sacrifice, of prayer, of the contrast between God and
Devil, of one omnipotent God, of a God-father, of a God-man, of
a Saviour, of an Avatar, of a Buddha, of a Messiah, of a Christ,

of salvation, of immortality, etc. It would be desirable to have some information on the development and history of the rational beings on other planets, and it is probable that in spite of many differences all the essential features of their spiritual and religious growth will prove the same. I am still convinced that the greater part of the parallelism between Buddhism and Christianity is of independent origin, for it is certain that at any rate the church development in both religions took place without any historical

THE ZODIAC ON THE MITHRAIC MONUMENT AT HEDDERNHEIM. [2514]

connection except in Tibet where the Nestorian faith had for a time taken deep root. And yet we have a Christian Doketism and a Buddhist Doketism; we have Christian reformers who believe in the paramount efficacy of faith, and Buddhist preachers who proclaim the doctrine almost in the same words as Luther, etc.

I believe that the decimal system of numbers originated naturally and necessarily, and it is obvious that it may very easily have developed simultaneously in perfect independence. If the rational

beings of some other planet have eight fingers, instead of ten, they
will with the same inevitable necessity develop an octonary system
which possesses many advantages over the decimal. Again, if they
had twelve fingers, they would count in dozens and dozens of dozens.

Some features are universal, others depend upon definite conditions, while all of them are subject to local modifications in un-

MAYAN CALENDAR.
Zejévary Manuscript.

essential details. Having gone in quest of unequivocal evidences
of the independent development of the universal, I found myself
everywhere baffled by a possible historical connection, and now I
am forced to concede that an interconnection of prehistoric mankind in its remotest corners can no longer be doubted.

Mr. Richard H. Geoghegan has published in *The Monist* (October 1906) an interesting article "On the Ideograms of the Chinese and Central American Calendars," in which he traces several most remarkable similarities between the Chinese and the Mayan calendars.

The results of Mr. Geoghegan's investigations suggest that in a prehistoric age there must have been an interconnection between

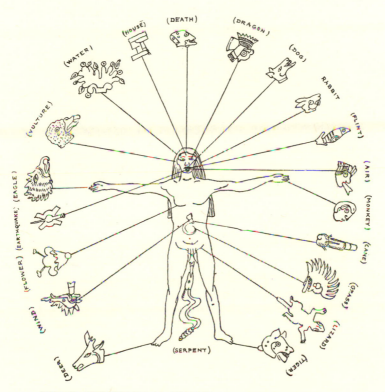

MAYAN ASSIGNMENT OF ANIMALS TO PARTS OF THE BODY. 4223

the primitive civilisation of America and Asia, and it can scarcely be gainsaid if we but compare the Mayan, the Chinese, and the mediæval European interpretation of the several organs of the body in terms of the calendar or the zodiac, and we must grant that here are similarities of such a peculiarly intricate character that they can not be explained as intrinsic in human nature, nor is it likely that the parallelism is accidental.

There can be no doubt that the entire Western civilisation may be traced to one common source. The Egyptians, the Greeks, and the Romans have inherited their mathematics, the division of the

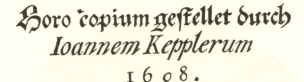

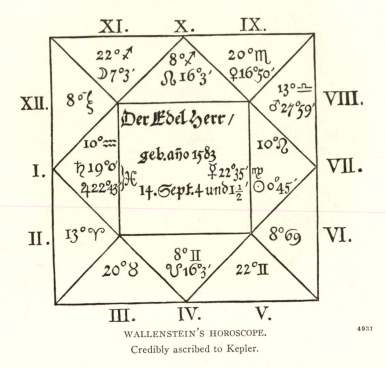

WALLENSTEIN'S HOROSCOPE.   4931
Credibly ascribed to Kepler.

day into twice twelve hours, and their calendars from ancient Babylonia, the influence of which has been preserved down to modern times, and can most palpably be recognised in astrology.

Astrology is unquestionably of Babylonian origin. It rests on the theory that the universe is a well-ordained whole governed by universal laws, and so the ancient sages assumed that life on earth is foreshadowed by the events in the celestial regions; and these notions adhered to the further development of astronomy with a persistence that is truly surprising.

Even as late as the fourteenth century astronomers were still

MEXICAN CALENDAR WHEEL.   4504

obliged to eke out a scant living with the help of astrology, and Kepler himself had to increase his means of subsistence by casting horoscopes. But he was great enough to take the situation humorously, and in one of his letters we read: "This astrology is indeed a foolish little daughter, but—*lieber Gott!*—where would her mother, the highly rational astronomy, be, if she did not have this foolish offspring? People are even more foolish, so foolish in fact, that this sensible old mother must for her own benefit cajole and deceive them through her daughter's foolish, idle talk."*

Europe has inherited its calendar with many incidental notions and superstitions from ancient Babylon. But back of the interconnection in historic ages there must have been a very intimate exchange of thought between the incipient civilisations of primitive China, of Babylon, and also of the American Maya. The American Maya must have brought many ideas along with them when they

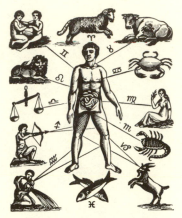

CHINESE ASSIGNMENT OF ANIMALS
4224   TO PARTS OF THE BODY.

EUROPEAN CONCEPTION OF
SIGNS OF THE ZODIAC   4184

settled in their new home which testifies to the hoariness of their culture.

At the time of the discovery of America they were far behind the Spaniards in the art of warfare, but they were their superiors in a proper calculation of the calendar. They divided their year into eighteen epochs of twenty days each with five intercalary days, but they knew also that this calculation was only approximate and had the difference adjusted before Pope Gregory's reform of the Julian calendar. But the point we wish to make here is not concerned with the sundry accomplishments of the Maya, but the remarkable

* See Carus Sterne's article "Copernicus, Tycho Brahe, and Kepler," *The Open Court,* XIV, 405.

similarities of detail between their symbolism and that of mediæval Europe as well as China.

In our researches we have never entered deeply into comparative astronomy, but judging from suggestions of scholars who have

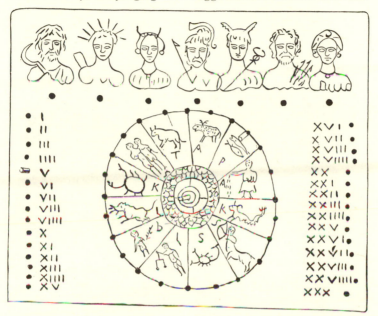

ROMAN CALENDAR STONE IN THE MUSEUM AT WÜRZBURG.
From *Weltall und Menschheit*, Vol. III, p. 19.

[The deities presiding over the seven days of the week are pictured on the top: Saturn for Saturday with sickle in hand; Mithra the sun-god, for Sunday; Diana, the moon-goddess, for Monday; Mars, (the Teutonic Tiu) for Tuesday; Mercury (the Teutonic Wodan) for Wednesday; Jupiter (the Teutonic Thor) for Thursday; Venus (Teutonic Frigga or Freya) for Friday. The circle represents the crude picture of the zodiac beginning at the top with *Aries,* and running around to the left, each sign being accompanied by the initial of its name.]

made a specialty of this interesting branch of human lore, we can say positively that the Babylonian origin of the division and names of the zodiac has been firmly established. Prof. Franz Boll has collected all pertinent material of Greek texts and also illustrations of several ancient representations of the starry heavens in his book,

Sphaera, neue griechische Texte und Untersuchungen zur Geschichte der Sternbilder (Leipsic, Teubner, 1903). He also refers to the method prevalent in Eastern Asia, of counting hours, months, and

2038   KUDURRU OF NAZI MARADAH, KING OF BABYLON, SON OF   2039
KURIGALZAR II.

[Most of the emblems are the same as in the preceding illustration except that the goddess Gula is here represented in full figure in a typical attitude with both hands raised.]

years by the duodenary system of animals and points out its similarities to the Babylonian system (pp. 326 ff.). Our own investi-

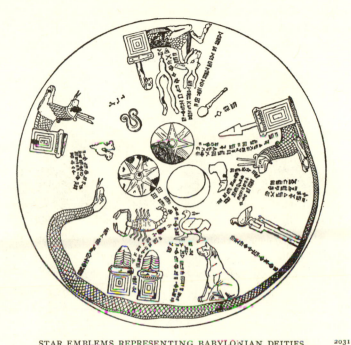

STAR EMBLEMS REPRESENTING BABYLONIAN DEITIES. 2031

CAP OF A KUDURRU.

[We see on the top sun, moon, and planet Venus, representing the Babylonian trinity of Shamash, Sin, and Istar. These three symbols are surrounded to the right of the moon by the lamp of the god Nusku, a goose-like bird, the scorpion, a double-headed symbol of un-known significance, a loop-like emblem and a stake bearing a tablet. The outer margin shows on the top the emblem of the ancient god Ea, a goat ending in a fish, a throne and a ram-headed mace; then turning to the right, we have the emblem of Marduk, a lance on a throne and the dragon Tiamat; further down an eagle (or a falcon) perched on a forked pole, a dog (or lion), two thrones with tiaras resting on them, and another throne, beside it lying an unknown scaled monster. The forked tree is the symbol of the goddess Nidaba, a form of Istar as the harvest goddess. The same deity is sometimes represented by an ear of wheat, in Hebrew *shibboleth* (from *shabal,* "to go forth, to sprout, to grow"); and judging from the pictures on the monuments, worshipers carried ears of wheat in their hands on the festival of the goddess. It is the same word which was used by Jeph-tha of Gilead to recognise the members of the tribe of Ephraim who pronounced it *sibboleth,* because they were unaccustomed to the sibi-lant *sh* (Judges xii. 6). From *shibboleth* the Latin word *Sybilla,* the name of the prophetess, the author of the Sybilline oracles, is derived. Nidaba's star is *Spica* (i. e., "ear of wheat,") the brightest star in the constellation *Virgo,* i. e., the virgin goddess Istar.]

gations corroborate Professor Boll's theory, and we owe to him a number of the illustrations here reproduced.

We complete the circle of evidences as to early prehistoric connections, by furnishing additional instances of pictures of the zodiac among other nations, that have been isolated for thousands of years.

The names of our own zodiac are commemorated in a couplet of two Latin hexameters as follows:

> "*Sunt Aries Taurus Gemini Cancer Leo Virgo*
> *Libraque Scorpius[1] Arcitenus[2] Caper[3] Amphora[4] Pisces,*

or in English: (1) the Ram, (2) the Bull, (3) the Twins, (4) the Crab, (5) the Lion, (6) the Virgin, (7) the Balance, (8) the Scorpion, (9) the Archer, (10) the Goat, (11) the Vase or Water-man, and (12) the Fishes.

All the zodiacs, together with their divisions into constellations, must have one common origin which can only have been in Babylon, the home of ancient astronomy. We possess among the cuneiform inscriptions of the first or second century B. C. some astronomical tablets which contain an enumeration of the Babylonian zodiac in abbreviations. They read as follows:[5]

1.	(*ku(sarikku)*)	= aries.
2.	(*te(mennu)*)	= taurus.
3.	(*mašu*)	= gemini.
4.	(*pulukku*)	= cancer.
5.	(*arū*)	= leo.
6.	(*serū*)	= virgo.
7.	(*zibanîtu*)	= libra.
8.	(*aqrabu*)	= scorpio.
9.	(*pa*)	= arcitenens.
10.	(*enzu*)	= caper.
11.	(*gu*)	= amphora [aquarius].
12.	(*zib*)	= pisces.

---

[1] "Scorpius" is commonly called *Scorpio;* the change in the ending is obviously made on account of the meter of the verse.

[2] Also commonly called *Sagittarius.*

[3] Also known under the name *Capricorn.*

[4] Also named *Aquarius.*

The identity of this series with our own and other zodiacs is most striking in the beginning, which like our own series starts with "The Ram," "The Bull," and "The Twins."

The constellations as represented on our modern globes are so outlined as to make the figures of the symbols cover the area of the stars, and the illustrators have adroitly utilised the stars as part of the picture. This method is according to an ancient tradition which can be traced back to antiquity and has produced the impression that the names of the constellations are due to the configuration of the stars. But while it is true that such names as "Charles's Wain" or "the Wagon" (in China called "the Bushel," in America "the Dipper") is a name apparently invented on account of the configuration of the stars, the same does not hold good for other constellations and least of all for the signs of the zodiac. In ancient Babylon, or even in ancient Akkad, certain names in the starry heavens were sacred to certain deities, and the names represented the several deities that presided over that part of the heavens. We must assume that in most cases the picture of a stellar configuration is a mere afterthought of the artist who tried to trace in it the deity or its symbol. We have in the zodiac and its names a grand religious world-conception which regards the entire cosmos as dominated by divine law, finding expression in divine power dominant according to a fixed constitution of the universe, rendering prominent in different periods definite divine influences represented as gods or archangels of some kind. Among them we notice one who appears as the omnipotent highest ruler, whose rank is analogous to a king of kings, for he governs the whole celestial world, and this highest ruler has been represented by different nations in different ways, and by kindred nations who followed kindred ideas in a kindred way. Thus we find the similarity of the highest god among the Assyrians and the Persians, and a close examination of the post-Exilic tendencies of Jewish history indicates that the Asur of the Assyrians so similar to Ahura Mazda of the Persians, is in all main features the same as Yahveh of the Jews.

---

[5] See Epping and Strassmaier, *Zeitschrift für Assyriologie,* Vol. V, Fascicle 4 (Oct. 1890, p. 351).

The idea that celestial conditions govern all earthly events is brought out very strongly in the Assyrian standards, which show the highest god Asur in the most conspicuous place, and in comparing his effigy to representations of Asur on the monuments, as well as to the modern illustrations of Sagittarius, we will be impressed with a strong similarity in these pictures.   The Assyrian

ANCIENT ASSYRIAN STANDARD.   4364

standards commonly show Asur as standing above a bull.   One very elaborate standard exhibits in addition to the god Asur, three symbols of the zodiac, which for some unknown reason, perhaps simply for the sake of symmetry, are duplicated.   There are two streams of water, two bulls, and two lion heads, and it is scarcely an accident that these symbols represent the Colures in about 3500

B. C. In the middle of the fourth millennium B. C. the solstitial
Colures lay in Aquarius and Leo, and the equinoctial Colures in
Taurus and Scorpio.[6]

If the god Asur, who is represented as an archer, stands for

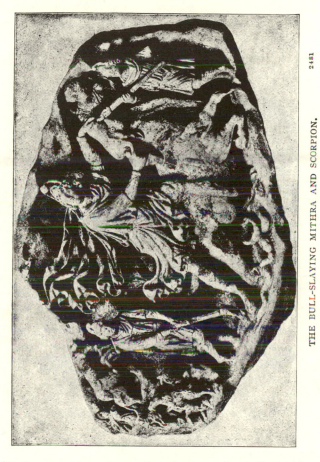

THE BULL-SLAYING MITHRA AND SCORPION.

2481

Sagittarius, we may assume that the two signs, *Sagittarius* and
Scorpio were originally one and became differentiated later on. We
shall present reasons, further down, which will make this assumption
probable.

[6] See also Plunket, *Ancient Calendars and Constellations,* Plate VIII.

Is it perhaps a reminiscence of kindred traditions when Mithra is pictured in the Mithraic monuments as slaying the divine bull? We notice in every one of the Mithra pictures the scorpion attacking the bull simultaneously with Mithra, and depriving him of his power of fecundation. *Scorpio* stands in opposition to *Taurus* and in winter nature loses its productivity. The same idea is suggested in the illustration of the crab on the kudurru pictured on page 106.

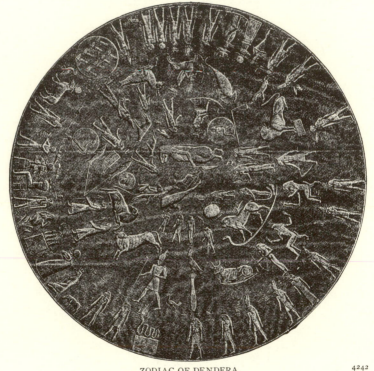

ZODIAC OF DENDERA.   4242

As to the identification of the Assyrian god Asur with the Persian Ahura, we will incidentally say that Professor Hommel goes so far as to maintain that Asur is merely the Assyrian pronunciation of the Elamitic "Ahura," and corroborates his statement by other examples. The Honorable Emmeline Mary Plunket makes this view her own and argues with great plausibility that

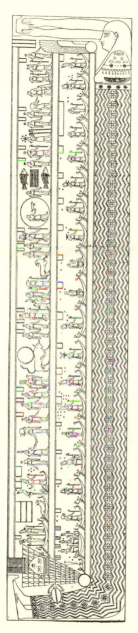

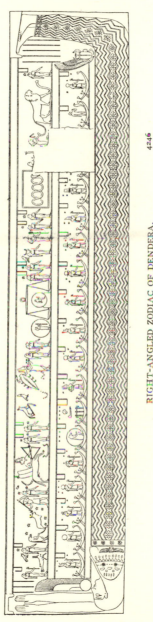

446

RIGHT-ANGLED ZODIAC OF DENDERA.

(On the next page we reproduce illustrations showing some details of this remarkable picture of the Egyptian zodiac which will serve as an evidence of the artistic elegance of the sculptor's work.)

an Elamite or Aryan race might have been in possession of Assyria at the time before the Semitic wave crowded the Elamites back farther north, and the Semitic settlers worshiped the god of the country in order to pacify his anger and keep on good terms with him. We know that in the same way the settlers of Samaria wor-

THE CONSTELLATION OF THE HAUNCH.*

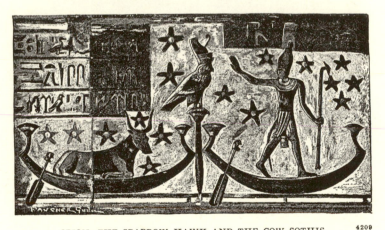

ORION, THE SPARROW HAWK AND THE COW SOTHIS.   4209

shiped the god of the Israelites in addition to their own gods, so as not to offend the divine power that governed the land.

*   *   *

The constellations of the zodiac were not invented simulta-

---

* Reproduced from Maspero, *Dawn of Civilization.*

neously with the division of the ecliptic into twelve mansions, for
many constellations of the ancient ecliptic are very irregular and

LATE ROMAN EGYPTIAN MARBLE PLAQUE.*   4243

[The center represents Apollo and Phœbe, the former with a solar
halo, the latter crowned with a crescent. Surrounding this are two
circles of twelve mansions each, the outer circle containing the signs
of the Greek zodiac, and the inner the corresponding signs of the
Egyptian zodiac. Beginning at the top the pictures run to the left as
follows: *Aries,* cat (inner circle) ; *Taurus,* jackal; *Gemini,* serpent;
Cancer, scarab; *Leo,* ass; *Virgo,* lion; *Libra,* goat; *Scorpio,* cow;
Sagittarius, falcon; *Capricorn,* baboon; *Aquarius,* ibis; *Pisces,* croco-
dile.]

reach in their bulk either above or below the exact path of the sun.
In fact, Eudoxus, Aratus, and Hipparchus do not enumerate twelve,

* Described by J. Daressy, *Recueil de travaux rel. à la philol, et à l'arch
Egypt. et Assyr.,* XXIII, 126 f.

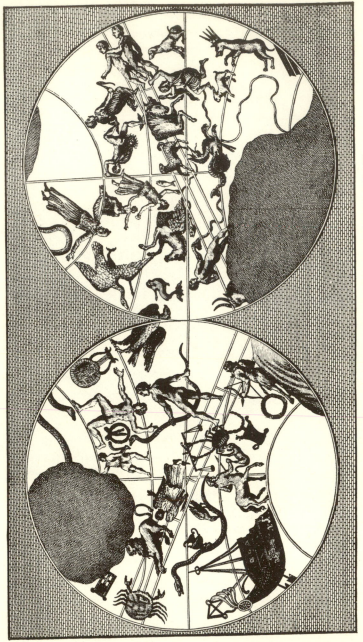

ROMAN GLOBE OF THE ECLIPTIC NOW IN THE FARNESIAN PALACE.

but only eleven constellations of the zodiac, and it seems that *Libra*, the Balance, is a later addition; and yet this change also is commonly supposed to have come from Babylon. We must conclude therefore that the constellations among the starry heavens were mapped out without special reference to the ecliptic, and are older. The irregularity of the Chinese constellations along the ecliptic, accordingly, would go far to prove that their names must have been imported into China before the ecliptic had finally been regulated into twelve equal mansions, each of 30 degrees.

Babylonian wisdom migrated in both directions, toward the east to China, and toward the west to Europe. It must have reached China at an early date in prehistoric times, and it has come down to us from the Greeks who in their turn received their information second hand through the Egyptians.

At every stage in this continuous transfer of ideas, the mythological names were translated into those that would best correspond to them. Istar changed to Venus, or *Virgo;* Bel Marduk to Zeus and Jupiter, and among the Teutons to Thor or Donar, etc.

During the Napoleonic expedition some interesting representations of the zodiac were discovered in the temple of the great Hathor at Dendera. They are not as old as was supposed in the first enthusiasm of their discovery for they were finished only under the first years of Nero; but they well represent the astronomical knowledge in Egypt which looks back upon a slow development for many centuries. We notice in the transition of the zodiac from Babylon to Egypt, and from Egypt to Greece, several changes of names which are still unexplained. Sirius is identified with Orion, and the Great Bear with Typhon, etc.

The Hindu* and the Arabian zodiacs are practically the same as ours, but the Chinese zodiac shows some deviations which, however, are too inconsiderable not to show plainly a common origin of the whole nomenclature.

The Arabian magic mirror, here reproduced, exhibits the twelve symbols of the zodiac in the outer circle, and the angels of the seven planets which preside also over the seven days of the week, appear

---

*For an illustration and description of the Hindu zodiacs see page 75.

in the inner circle. The center where we would expect some emblem of the sun shows the picture of an owl.

It is interesting to see how sometimes the external shape of a figure is preserved, sometimes the name. We find for instance the Archer (called *Sagittarius* or *Arcitenus*) represented as a double-

ANCIENT ARABIAN ZODIAC (13th CENT.)   4205

[Engraved on a magic mirror. Dedicated as the inscription reads "To the Sovereign Prince Abulfald, Victorious Sultan, Light of the World."]

headed centaur drawing a bow in almost the same outlines on an ancient Babylonian kudurru, as in modern charts of the heavens. And it is noteworthy that in Greece, too, this centaur, in a note of Teukros, is spoken of a two-faced (διπρόσωπος). In the same way the scorpion-man holds the bow, and he again resembles the outlines of the scorpion, so as to indicate that the bow has taken the place of the claws. Notice further that the ancient picture of the Babylonian *Sagittarius* possesses two tails, one like that of a horse, the other of the same form as that of both the scorpion-man and the scorpion. All this suggests that the two emblems, *Sagittarius* and *Scorpio* which are neighbors in the zodiac, may originally have been one and were differentiated in the course of time, in order to make the mansions of equal length.

In this connection we would also remind our readers of the obvious similarity between the picture of the god Asur and *Sagittarius*. But even differences are instructive and there can be no doubt that they suggest prehistoric connections between the far East and the West.

The symbol of the ancient god Ea is a goat terminating in a

THE EMBLEM OF EA.   4198
[Babylonian Symbol of Capricorn.]

fish. The corresponding sign of the zodiac which in Europe is regarded as a goat and called *Caper* or *Capricorn,* is considered a fish in China and called "the Dolphin." In a similar way the division of the zodiac that was originally connected with the annual inundation in Babylonia, is called either *Aquarius* or *Amphora* and is represented in the Chinese zodiac as a vase; in Western charts as a man holding an urn pouring forth water.

The astronomical knowledge of Babylon migrated west by way of Egypt and Greece, to modern Europe, and on its way east it must have reached China at a very early date.

It is not our intention to follow here all the changes which the zodiac underwent in different countries. It is sufficient to call attention to the undeniable similarity of all of them. It would take

the concentration of a specialist for every change to point out the
modifications which the several signs underwent in their transference

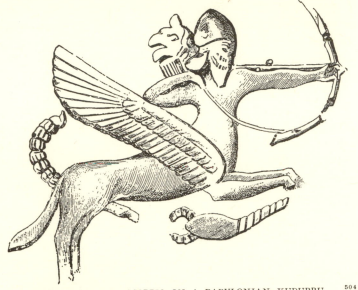

SAGITTARIUS AND SCORPIO ON A BABYLONIAN KUDURRU. 504

SCORPION-MAN AND SCORPION. 4241

from place to place and from nation to nation. One instance will
be sufficient to show how the names with their peculiar associations

affected the interpretation of the several constellations among the different nations.

Cancer was called "the scarab" by the Egyptians, and was endowed with special sanctity for the deep religious significance of the scarab in Egypt is well known.

The scarab (*ateuchus sacer*) is an Egyptian bug which belongs to the same family as our June bug, the cockchafer, and the tumble-bug. In habits it is most like the latter, for like her the female scarab deposits her eggs in a lump of mud which she reduces to the shape of a ball. The ancient Egyptians did not distinguish between the male and the female scarab, and had not watched how they deposited and laid their eggs, so it happened that when they witnessed the mysterious bug rolling a mud ball along the road, they were under the impression that the scarab renewed his existence by some mysterious means, and possessed the divine power of resurrection from the dust of the earth. Accordingly the scarab became in Egyptian mythology the symbol of creation and immortality. The sacredness of the symbol was for a long time preserved in the ancient Christian churches, for Christ is repeatedly called "the Scarab."

The passages on the subject have been collected by Mr. Isaac Myer, who says:[9]

"After the Christian era the influence of the cult of the scarab was still felt. St. Ambrose, Archbishop of Milan, calls, Jesus, 'The good Scarabæus, who rolled up before him the hitherto unshapen mud of our bodies.'[10] St. Epiphanius has been quoted as saying of Christ: 'He is the Scarabæus of God,' and indeed it appears likely that what may be called Christian forms of the scarab, yet exist. One has been described as representing the crucifixion of Jesus. It is white and the engraving is green, and on the back are two palm branches. Many others have been found apparently engraved with the Latin cross."[11]

While the Babylonian, or rather Akkadian, origin of the Chi-

[9] *Scarabs.* London: D. Nutt.
[10] *Works,* Paris, 1686. Vol. I, col. 1528, No. 113. *Egyptian Mythology and Egyptian Christianity.* By Samuel Sharpe, London, 1863, p. 3.
[11] *An Essay on Scarabs,* by W. J. Loftie, B.A., F.S.A., pp. 58, 59.

nese zodiac must be regarded as an established fact, we can not deny that it possesses some peculiarities of its own.

The Chinese begin the enumeration of their zodiac with a

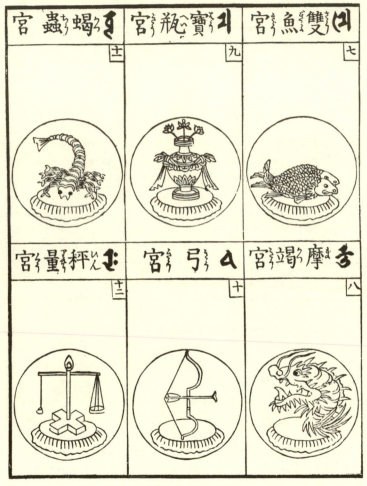

CHINESE ZODIAC.

constellation called "Twin Women," which corresponds to our *Virgo,* whence they count in an inverse order, (2) the Lion, (3) the Crab, (4) Man and Woman (answering to our *Gemini*), (5) the Bull,

(6) the Ram, (7) the Fishes, (8) the Dolphin (*Capricorn*), (9) the Vase (*Aquarius*), (10) the Bow (*Sagittarius*), (11) the Scorpion, and (12) the Balance.

CHINESE ZODIAC.

It is noteworthy that the Chinese and Hindu zodiacs agree in representing *Gemini* as a man and woman, while in all Western

almanacs they are represented as brothers which is probably due
to their identification with Castor and Pollux.

The zodiac corresponds closely to the twelve mansions of the
ecliptic which are called in China as follows:

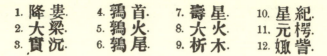

These names in a literal translation mean:

1. Descending misfortune,
2. Large beam,
3. Kernel sunk,
4. Quail's head,
5. Quail's fire,
6. Quail's tail,

7. Longevity star,
8. Great fire,
9. Split wood,
10. Stellar era,
11. Original hollow,
12. Bride defamed.

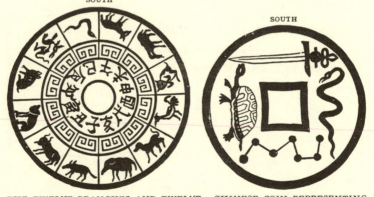

THE TWELVE BRANCHES AND TWELVE
ANIMALS REPRESENTING THE
TWELVE MANSIONS.
4206

CHINESE COIN REPRESENTING
SYMBOLS OF THE FOUR
QUARTERS.*
4207

We have translated these names for the convenience of the
English reader, but must warn him that their significance has
nothing to do with either the astronomical or astrological meaning
of these terms.

---

* We will add that the usual way of symbolising the four quarters is east
by the azure dragon, north by the sombre warrior, south by the vermillion
bird, and west by the white tiger. Compare Mayers, *Ch. R. M.* II, 91.

TABLE OF THE TWELVE HOURS

| HOUR | POPULAR NAME | ANIMAL NAME | RELATION TO THE ZODIAC | | RELATION TO THE ECLIPTIC |
			CHINESE	EUROPEAN	
11 P. M. - 1 A. M.	Midnight	Rat	Vase	Aquarius	Original Hollow
1 A. M. - 3 A. M.	Hour of the Crowing Rooster	Bull	Dolphin	Capricorn	Stellar Era
3 A. M. - 5 A. M.	Dawn	Tiger	Bow	Sagittarius	Split Wood
5 A. M. - 7 A. M.	Sunrise	Hare	Scorpion	Scorpio	Great Fire
7 A. M. - 9 A. M.	Breakfast Time	Dragon	Balance	Libra	Longevity Star
9 A. M. -11 A. M.	Forenoon	Serpent	Twin Sisters	Virgo	Quail's Tail
11 A. M. - 1 P. M.	Midday	Horse	Lion	Leo	Quail's Fire
1 P. M. - 3 P. M.	Early Afternoon	Lamb	Crab	Cancer	Quail's Head
3 P. M. - 5 P. M.	Late Afternoon	Monkey	Man and Woman	Gemini	Kernel Sunk
5 P. M. - 7 P. M.	Sunset	Rooster	Bull	Taurus	Large Beam
7 P. M. - 9 P. M.	Twilight	Dog	Ram	Aries	Descending Misfortune
9 P. M. -11 P. M.	Hour of Rest	Boar	Fishes	Pisces	Bride Defamed

The twelve mansions as well as the twelve double-hours are closely related to the twelve animals, the rat representing north, or midnight; the goat, south; the hare, east; the cock, west.

The Chinese, like the Babylonians, divide the day into double hours which according to the notions of Chinese occultism have definite relations to the twelve signs of the zodiac and the twelve mansions of the ecliptic, as explained in the adjoined table.

It seems strange to us that the wise men of the prehistoric ages in Babylonia and Egypt, in China and Central America, troubled themselves so much about the zodiac and the calendar, but we will understand their solicitude when we consider that their world-conception was based upon the idea of cosmic law. They thought that the universe was dominated by conditions which were pre-determined by the events that took place in the starry heavens and would in some way be repeated in this and the nether world. This was the bottom rock on which rested their religion, their philosophy, and their ethics. The polytheistic mythology is merely the poetic exterior of this view, and the astrological superstitions that grow from it, its wild excrescences. We need not be blind to the many errors and absurdities of the ancient occultism to understand and grant the truth that underlies its system. This fundamental truth is the universality of law; a firm belief that the world is a cosmos, an orderly whole dominated by definite leading principles; the con-viction that our destiny, the fate of both nations and individuals is not a product of chance, but determined according to a divine plan in systematic regularity.

Occultism may now be an aberration, a survival of antiquated views, but there was a time when it was the stepping-stone of primi-tive man to a higher and deeper and truer interpretation of the world.

We would not possess astronomy to-day had not our ancestors been given to astrology, and in the same way all our science, phi-losophy and religion has grown out of the past and we are more indebted to the half-truths of the antiquated world-conception than we are commonly inclined to admit.

A THRONELESS KING AND HIS EMPIRE.

CONFUCIUS.

THE moral teacher of China, the man who gave definite form to Chinese ethics and has molded the character of the nation, was K'ung-tze, or K'ung fu tze, which has been Latinised into "Confucius." The word *K'ung* (which literally translated means "hole") is his family name, *tze* designates him as a philosopher, while *fu* is a title of respect.

Confucius was born in the year 550 B. C.[1] in Tsou, a township of the district of Ch'ang-Ping, which is the modern Szu Shui in the province Shantung.[2] He is descended from a distinguished family of officers.[3] His great grandfather had come from the state Sung during a feud with a powerful enemy, to seek refuge in the state Lu, and his father whose full name was K'ung Shu Liang Ho, having had nine daughters from his first wife and a crippled son from a concubine, married again at the advanced age of seventy

---

[1] According to Sse Ma T'sien, Confucius was born in the twenty-second year of duke Hsiang of Lu, which is the year 550 B. C. This statement is adopted by Chu Hsi in his *Biography of Confucius* which prefaces the standard edition of the Lun Yü, but there is no unanimity as to the exact date for the commentators Ku' Liang and Kung Yang place his birth in the year 552 B. C., and even they do not agree as to the month. Ku' Liang states that Confucius was born on the twenty-first day of the tenth month of the twenty-first year of the Duke Hsiang of Lu, which was the twentieth year of the Emperor Ling. While Kung Yang agrees in all other details, he states that it was the eleventh and not the tenth month.

[2] There is no unanimity as to the place of Confucius's birth. At present there are two towns that make rival claims for the honor. The other one not mentioned in the text is Yen Chou also situated in Shantung.

[3] Details of the family history of Confucius are reported by Legge in his edition of *The Chinese Classics,* I, pp. 56 ff.

STAIRWAY OF THE TEMPLE OF CONFUCIUS AT PEKING. 311

the youngest daughter of the Yen family, called Cheng Tsai; and when a son was born to them, they called him Ch'iu, i. e., "hill," because, as the legend relates, the babe's forehead bulged out in a hill-like protuberance. This K'ung Ch'iu was destined to become the ideal of China, Confucius.

K'ung Shu, the father, died three years after the birth of his son, and the widow moved with her child to a village in the district Ch'ü Fou.

Many stories of miraculous occurrences are told of the birth of Confucius. In one of them we are told that the marvelous animal, called *lin,* brought a tablet to Cheng Tsai, the sage's mother, on which this prophecy was written:

"The son of the essence of water [i. e., the principle of purity] shall come forth at the decay of the Chow [dynasty] and he shall be a throneless king."

Most of the birthstories of the sage are of later origin and show Buddhist influence. They were invented because the followers of Confucius did not want to see their founder outdone in honors, and so they vied with Buddhist traditions in claiming a supernatural origin for their great sage as well.

Nothing is known of the childhood of Confucius except that he was distinguished by a serious disposition and showed in his games an extreme fondness for rituals and ceremonies.

At the age of nineteen he married, and when a son was born to him he called him Li, which means "carp." He entered public service as a controller of public granaries, while his virtuous deportment, his admiration of the ancient sages, and his inclination to moralise, attracted general attention so as to surround him with a number of admirers who looked up to him as their master. We owe it to his disciples that his principles and moral maxims became known to posterity and were cherished by the Chinese nation. Confucius himself never wrote a work on his doctrines, and he characterised himself as "a transmitter, not an originator,"[4] but his faithful disciples compiled a book of reminiscences which they published under the title *Lún Yü,* "Conversations and Sayings," which in the English-speaking world is best known as *Confucian Analects.*

---

[4] *Analects,* VII, i.

It has become one of the most important canonical books of China and is regarded as a reliable authority for rules of conduct.

In 527 Cheng Tsai, the mother of Confucius, died, and he had both his parents buried together in Fang, his father's former home, under one tumulus.

The *Confucian Analects* are not a systematic treatise on ethics, but have the appearance of mere anecdotes, being sayings of the master, mostly introduced by the simple words "The Master said," and sometimes mentioning the occasion on which certain sayings

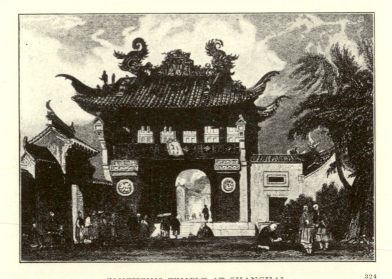

CONFUCIUS TEMPLE AT SHANGHAI.   324

of his had been uttered. Confucius was an extremely conservative man and his ideal lay in the past. The great patterns of conduct were the sages of yore, and he selected from them as models of conduct the most famous rulers, such as Yao, Shun, the Duke of Chou, and King Wan.

Confucius is frequently represented as a rationalist whose religion, if it may be called so, consisted purely of practical considerations of life. But this is not quite true, for his belief in mysticism is fully demonstrated by his reverence for the *Yih King,* the canonical book of mystic lore of China, with reference to which he said in his advanced age: "If some years could be added to my life, I would give fifty of them to the study of the Book of Changes, for then I would have avoided great errors."

Confucius is credibly believed to be the author of an appendix to the *Yih King,* the Book of Changes, called "The Ten Wings," which proves that this ancient document was to him as enigmatical as it remained to all succeeding generations.

In order to study the archives of antiquity, Confucius went to the capital of the empire, the city of Lo, where the most famous thinker of the age, Lao Tan, better known under the title Lao Tze (i. e., "the old philosopher") held the position of keeper of the archives. The story has it that these two great representatives of a radically opposed conception of life met personally, but their interview was not satisfactory to either. Lao Tze insisted on simplicity of the heart and expected that manners and rituals would adjust themselves, while Confucius proposed to train mankind to genuine virtue and especially to filial piety by punctilious observance of the rules of propriety. The interview is recorded by Ssu Ma Hsien, and has been retold with literary embellishments by the great Taoist litterateur Chuang Tze.

Confucius taught the Golden Rule in these words:

I so pu yü, mo shi yü jen.

己所不欲 勿施於人

"What ye will not have done to you, do ye not unto others."

The fame of Confucius had gradually spread throughout the country, and the sovereign of his native state, Duke Ting of Lu, made him chief magistrate of a town in which he was to try his principles of government. Confucianists claim that he worked a marvelous reformation in the manners of the people, and so his sovereign raised him to a higher position, entrusting him first with the ministry of works, and then with the ministry of justice.

In his fifty-seventh year Confucius withdrew from public office in order to show his disapproval of the conduct of his sovereign. The Confucianist report states that a neighboring prince, the Duke of Ch'i, envied the Duke Ting because of his famous minister, and in order to alienate his affections from the sage, he sent to the court of Lu a present of eighty beautiful maidens and thirty spans of horses, thereby reclaiming Ting's preference for sport and frivolities. The resignation of the sage did not, however, have the desired effect. The Duke appointed another minister of justice from among the great number of office seekers, while the sage now traveled from state to state in the hope of finding another dignified employment as adviser to a ruler who would venture to introduce the principles of his system of morality, and restore the ideal of China's glorious past in his government.

The time of his travels was a long series of disappointments to Confucius. He was received sometimes with honors and sometimes with indifference, but there was no prince who was willing to give him the desired employment. His enforced leisure was well utilised in literary labors, for Confucius collected a number of writings which he deemed worthy of preservation. They constitute now the second portion of the canonical scriptures of China, and have as such the title *King,* i. e., "canon," or "authoritative books." The only original work he ever composed is a history of his native state beginning in the year 722 B. C., which is called "Spring and Autumn," being a poetical title to indicate the succession of the seasons and the events belonging thereto. He was not a historian, however, for he simply chronicled successive happenings without pointing out their historical connection.

The older Confucius grew the more disappointed was he that his life should have been spent in vain. We are told in the Lun Yü that he said:

"No wise ruler rises; no one in the empire will make me his master. My time has come to die."

Saddened by the fact that his moral views were rejected by the princes of the nation, he predicted the coming of turbulent times and civil wars, events which had indeed become unavoidable through the degeneration of many petty courts and their disregard for the welfare of the people.

Once it happened (so Kung Yang informs us)[5] that a strange creature had been killed on a hunt of the Duke Ai of Lu, and the sage was called to inspect the body and give his opinion. Confucius declared it to be that supernatural animal called Lin, the appearance of which is deemed a rare occurrence. In his despair Confucius looked upon the death of this royal beast as a bad omen and he exclaimed: "My teaching is finished indeed."*

It is pathetic to observe the sage's despair at the end of his career; but such is the fate of reformers and this saying of Confucius sounds very much like a literal version of Christ's last word, "It is finished!"

Two years later Confucius felt the approach of his end. While he walked in front of his house he muttered this verse:

哲	梁	泰
人	木	山
其	其	其
萎	壞	頹
乎	乎	乎

"Huge mountains wear away.
          Alas!
The strongest beams decay.
          Alas!
And the sage like grass
Must fade. Alas!"

[The original is quoted from *Li Ki,* "The Book of Ritual."]

These lines of complaint are the *Eli Eli, lama sabachthani* of Confucius. He feels forsaken and fears that his work has been in vain.

Confucius died in 478 in retirement, and his faithful followers built a tomb over his remains, mourning on the spot for three years. His most devoted admirer, Tze Kung, built a hut and lived there for three years longer.

The fame of Confucius did not spread beyond a limited circle of disciples until a new period of prosperity began to dawn on China, which took place in the rise of the Han dynasty. Kao Tsou, the first Han emperor, was an admirer of the Confucian ideal. He visited the sage's tomb in 195 and offered there sacrifices to his memory. He had his books re-edited and ordered them to be carefully preserved.

---

[5] Kung Yang is one of the three commentators of Kung Tse's historical book *Spring and Autumn,* the others being Tso Chi and Ku Liang.

* This is a verbatim translation of the four words *wu tao ch'iung i.*

Further honors were heaped upon Confucius when the emperor P'ing Ti had a temple erected to his memory and raised him to the dignity of a duke, conferring on him the official name, "Duke Ni, the Perfect and Illustrious." This occurred in the year one of the Christian era.

In 739 the Emperor Hsüan T'sung canonised him under the title "Prince of Illustrious Learning" and made him the object of veneration in the official ceremonies of the government.

Twice a year a special day is set aside for the worship of Confucius, and it is an established custom that at the imperial college the emperor himself attends the festival in state. Bowing his head six times to the ground, he invokes the spirit of the sage in a kneeling position with these words (quoted in Legge's translation):

> "Great art thou, O perfect sage!
> Thy virtue is full; thy doctrine complete.
> Among mortal men there has not been thine equal.
> All kings honor thee.
> Thy statutes and laws have come gloriously down.
> Reverently have the sacrificial vessels been set out.
> Full of awe, we sound our drums and bells."

In addition to the books which Confucius had compiled there are two more writings on his system of ethics, which have acquired canonical authority. Both breathe the spirit of the great master and are written in a simple direct style of pure ethics founded upon the principles of filial piety, without any reference to religious or metaphysical motives. They are the "Great Learning" (*Ta Hsiao*) and "Middle Doctrine" (*Chung Yung*).

Children are taught from a tender age to reverence Confucius, and every school in China possesses his picture before which teachers and scholars pay homage to the sage.

Whatever opinion we may have of Confucius, one thing stands out clearly, indicated by the great significance he holds in the history of China, in Chinese literature, and in Chinese thought: viz., that he has been and still is the greatest exponent of the Chinese national character; for his ideals as well as his attitude toward life are typically Chinese.

Confucius was a throneless king indeed, and his empire is the realm of moral aspirations wherever Chinese civilisation has taken root. The emperor, as well as the entire machinery of the Chinese government is but the organ of the Chinese spirit,—the executor

A CHILD WORSHIPING THE SAGE. 2317

cf ideas which determine the character of the nation, and this spirit, the genius of the Chinese nation, is Confucius. His domain is the social order of the empire, the administration from the throne down to its lowliest subject, and especially the schools. Confucius is worshiped as the incarnation of morality.

FILIAL PIETY.

Several years ago while sauntering through the Pan-American Exposition at Buffalo, New York, my eye was attracted by a little Chinese store where, among other Oriental curios, were displayed wall pendants, ornamental mottoes designed to be hung up as decorations in the sitting-rooms of the Celestials. Being interested in the subject of things Chinese I secured copies of them,

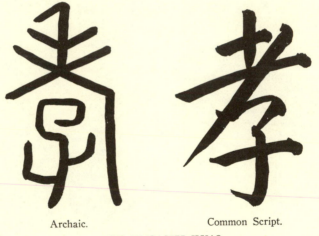

Archaic.   Common Script.

5091   THE CHARACTER HSIAO.   5090

and since they are characteristic of the spirit of Chinese moralism, I take pleasure in reproducing them here, for, indeed, our description of Chinese thought would not be complete without a reference to Chinese ethics in which the ideal of *hsiao,* i. e., filial piety, plays so prominent a part.

The paper and art work of these pendants are crude enough to allow the assumption that the prints must be very cheap in China, and designed for the common people and not for the rich. Probably they cost not more than one or two cents apiece in Peking or Hong Kong, and evidently serve the two purposes of instruction and ornament.

The Chinese are much more of a moralising people than we are; for while we dislike abstract moralising, they delight in it and do not tire of impressing upon their children the praiseworthiness of filial devotion.

The character *hsiao* consists of two symbols representing a child supporting an old man, which means that children should honor and care for parents in their old age, and filial piety is supposed to be the basis of all virtue. The moral relations are regarded

Ornamental.   Seal Style.

5089   5088

THE CHARACTER HSIAO.

as mere varieties of *hsiao;* and the original significance of the word, which means chiefly the devotional attitude of a child toward his parents, includes such relations as the obedience of the subject to his ruler, of the wife to her husband, of the younger brother to his elder brother, and of any one's relations to his superiors, including especially man's relation to Heaven or the Lord on High, to God.

The Chinese ornament their rooms, not as we do with pictures of beauty, but with moral sayings; and the two here reproduced are typical of the national character of the Chinese. The former of the two pendants, literally translated, reads:

父子協力山成玉

"When father | and son | combine | their efforts | mountains | are changed | into gems."

The saying, however, is not an admonition to parents to keep in harmony with their sons but to sons to be obedient to their parents.

The second pendant reads:

兄弟同心土變金

"When elder brother | and younger brother (or briefly, when brothers) | are harmonious | in their hearts | the earth | will be changed | into an Eldorado."[1]

It will be noticed that the letters are pictures containing figures and Chinese characters; and we have here the Chinese peculiarity of utilising their script for illustrations which represent scenes from well-known Chinese stories of filial devotion; all of them being taken from a famous book called *Twenty-four Stories of Filial Devotion.* These stories are known to every Chinaman, for they form the most important text-book of their moral education.

The first character (*fu,* meaning "father") represents Wang Ngai, who lived during the Wei dynasty (220-364 A. D.). His mother was much afraid of lightning and so during thunderstorms stood greatly in need of her son's comfort. The story tells us that after her death Wang Ngai continued to show his devotion by visiting her tomb, whenever a thunder-cap appeared on the horizon. The picture shows him bringing offerings to her grave and protecting it against the fury of the thunder-god, who is seen hovering above him in the air. (No. 805*a,* p. 242.[2])

The inscription of the second character (*tze,* meaning "son") reads in one place "Tai Son's aged mother," and in another "Tan Hsiang's daughter weeping over a sweet melon."

The third character (*hsieh,* meaning "combine") pictures a child standing before an old gentleman. The inscription reads:

---

[1] Literally, gold.

[2] The numbers and pages in parentheses refer to Mayers, *Chinese Reader's Manual.*

fu
[When] father

tze
[and] sons

hsieh
combine

li
[their] efforts

shan
mountains

ch'êng
are fashioned

yü
into gems.

hsiung
[When] elder brothers

ti
[and] younger brothers

t'ung
[are] harmonious

hsin
[in their] hearts

t'u
the earth

pien
is changed

chin
into an Eldorado (gold).

"Keeping in his bag a crab apple he showed his devotion to his parent." It refers to the story of Luh Sü. When a boy of six years he visited Yen Yü who gave him crab apples to eat but noticed that the child kept one in his bag for his mother. (No. 443, p. 140.)

The fourth character (*li,* meaning "strength") illustrates the story of Hwang Hiang who, as a boy of seven, after his mother's death devoted himself unweariedly to his father's comfort. In summer he fanned his pillow, in winter he kept it warm. (No. 217, pp. 69-70.)

The fifth character (*shan,* meaning "mountain") represents Kiang Keh, a Chinese Anchises of about 490 A. D. Once he rescued his mother during a disturbance of the peace by carrying her many miles on his shoulders. Behind the fugitives in the center of the character rages the spirit of rebellion and in the right-hand corner is seen a deserted house. (No. 255, p. 80.)

The sixth character (*ch'êng,* meaning "fashioning, shaping, transforming") illustrates the story of Wu Meng who exposes himself to the bites of mosquitoes lest his mother be stung by them. The picture of the hero of the story lying naked on a couch is not very clear in the reproduction, but the comfort of his mother, reclining in an easy chair finds a distinct expression. (No. 808, p. 260.)

The last character (*yü*) of the first series is remarkable in so far as it stands for the only instance of a woman's being praised for filial devotion. It represents Ts'ui She who nursed at her own breast her toothless old mother-in-law who was incapable of taking other nourishment. (No. 791*a,* p. 238.)

The first character of the second pendant (*hsiung,* meaning "elder brother") relates to Wang Siang, whose stepmother felt an appetite for fresh fish in winter. He went out on the river, lay down on the ice, warming it with his own body, and caught a couple of carp, which he presented to her. (No. 816, p. 241.)

The next character (*ti,* "younger brother") shows the famous Emperor Yao in the center and before him his successor Shun, the pattern of filial as well as royal virtues. The elephant, one of the animals that helped him plow the fields, is visible above Shun on the right-hand side. William Frederick Mayers in his *Chinese Reader's Manual* (No. 617, p. 189) says about him:

"Tradition is extremely discordant with reference to his origin and descent. According to the Main Records of the five Emperors, his personal name was Ch'ung Hwa, and he was the son of Ku Sow, a reputed descendant of the emperor Chwan Hü. (He had also the designation Yü, which is by some referred to a region in modern Ho-nan, but by others to the territory of Yü Yao, in modern Che-kiang, with one or the other of which it is sought to connect him.) His father, Ku Sow (lit. 'the blind old man') on the death of Shun's mother, took a second wife, by whom he had a son named Siang; and preferring the offspring of his second union to his eldest son, he repeatedly sought to put the latter to death. Shun, however, while escaping this fate, in no wise lessened his dutiful conduct toward his father and stepmother, or his fraternal regard for Siang. He occupied himself in ploughing at Li Shan, where his filial piety was rewarded by beasts and birds who spontaneously came to drag his plough and to weed his fields. He fished in the Lui Lake and made pottery on the banks of the Yellow River. Still his parents and his brother sought to compass his death; but although they endeavored to make him perish by setting fire to his house and by causing him to descend a deep well, he was always miraculously preserved. In his twentieth year, he attracted by his filial piety the notice of the wise and virtuous Yao, who bestowed upon him his two daughters in marriage, and disinherited his son Chu of Tan, in order to make Shun his successor upon the throne. In the 71st year of his reign (B. C. 2287), Yao associated his protégé with him in the government of the empire, to which the latter succeeded on the death of Yao in B. C. 2258."

The character *t'ung,* which means "agree," refers to Meng Tsung of the third century A. D., whose mother loved to eat bamboo shoots. While he was sorrowing because they do not sprout in winter, the miracle happened that in spite of the frost the bamboos began to put forth their sprouts, and so he was enabled to fulfil his mother's desire. (No. 499, p. 155.) The picture shows a table on which the dish of bamboo sprouts is served, the face of his mother

hovering above it. On the right hand Meng Tsung sits sorrowing;
the left-hand stroke is a sprouting bamboo stick.

Yen-Tze, the hero of the next story, depicted in the character
"heart," is said to have ministered to his mother's preference for
the milk of the doe by disguising himself in a deer skin and mingling
with a herd of deer in the forest, where he succeeded in milking a
doe and in spite of robbers, represented as attacking him on either
side, he carried his mother's favorite food safely home in a pail. (No.
916, p. 276.)

The character *t'u,* "earth," depicts the touching story of the
sacrifice of Yang Hiang, who saw a tiger approaching his father
and threw himself between him and the beast. (No. 882, p. 266.)
In the reproduction it is difficult to recognise the crouching tiger,
which forms the stroke through the character.

The next to the last character (*pien,* meaning "changes") refers
to Min Sun, a disciple of Confucius. Mayers says: "His stepmother,
it is recorded, having two children of her own, used him ill and
clothed him only in the leaves of plants. When this was discovered
by his father, the latter became wroth and would have put away
the harsh stepmother, but Min Sun entreated him saying: 'It is
better that one son should suffer from cold than three children be
motherless!' His magnanimous conduct so impressed the mind of
his stepmother that she became filled with affection toward him."
(No. 503, p. 156.)

The last character (*chin,* meaning "gold") bears the inscription
"With mulberries he shows his filial devotion to his mother." It illustrates the story of Ts'ai Shun who during the famine caused by
the rebellion of Wang Meng (25 A. D.) picked wild mulberries in
the woods and brought the black ones to his mother while he was
satisfied with the unripe yelow ones. The picture shows a robber
watching the boy. In China even criminals have respect for the
devotion of children to their parents. So in recognition of his filial
piety the robber made him a present of rice and meat.

We here reproduce a series of illustrations representing the
twenty-four well-known stories of filial devotion, which, however,
we regret to say are not by a Chinese illustrator but by one of the

most remarkable artists of Japan, Hokusai, the painter of the poor. Crude woodcut reproductions of these pictures are known all over the country of the rising sun.

They represent (beginning always with the picture in the right-hand upper corner and proceeding downward) :

1. Shun, the person mentioned above destined to become the son-in-law and successor of Emperor Yao, assisted in his plowing by an elephant.

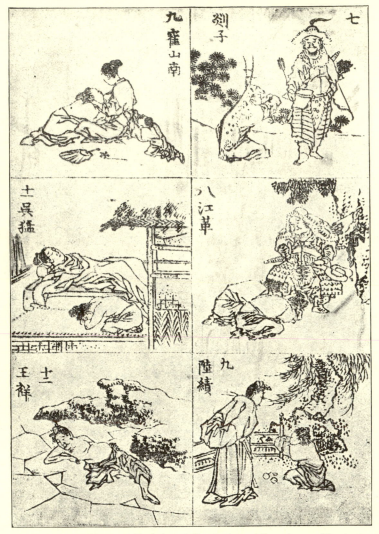

2. Tseng Shen, a disciple of Confucius. The picture illustrates a miraculous event. When he was gathering fuel in the woods,

his mother, in her anxiety to see him, bit her finger; and such was the sympathy between the two that he was aware of his mother's desire and at once appeared in her presence. (No. 739, p. 223.)

3. Wen Ti, natural son of Kao Tsu, founder of the Han dynasty, succeeded to the throne after the usurpation by the Empress Dowager in 179 B. C. When his mother fell sick he never left her apartment for three years and did not even take time to change his apparel. He is also famous as a most humane monarch.

4. Min Sun, maltreated by his stepmother, has been mentioned above. (No. 503, p. 156.)

5. Chung Yeo, another disciple of Confucius, famous for his martial accomplishments, who died a hero's death in the suppression of a rebellion. He used to say: "In the days when I was poor I carried rice upon my back for the support of those who gave me birth; and now, for all that I would gladly do so again, I cannot recall them to life!" (No. 91, pp. 29-30.)

6. Tung Yung was too poor to give his father a decent burial. So he bonded himself for 10,000 pieces of cash to perform the funeral rites with all propriety. "When returning to his home, he met a woman who offered herself as his wife, and who repaid the loan he had incurred with 300 webs of cloth. The pair lived happily together for a month, when the woman disclosed the fact that she was no other than the star Chih Nü,[1] who had been sent down by the Lord of Heaven, her father, to recompense an act of filial piety; and saying this she vanished from his sight." (No. 691, p. 210.)

7. The story of Yen-Tze, who while dressed in a deer-skin, is here pictured as meeting a robber. (No. 916, p. 276.)

8. Kiang Keh asking the robber chief's permission to allow him to carry away his mother. (No. 255, p. 80.)

9. Luh Sü (who lived in the first century of the Christian era), was liberated by his jailer, when imprisoned for complicity in a conspiracy, on account of the devotion he showed toward his mother. (No. 443, p. 140.)

10. The story of Ts'ui She, nursing her husband's mother.

---

[1] The star Vega, a in Lyre. The fairy story which the Chinese tell in connection with this star is given on page 77.

11. Wu Meng (No. 868, p. 260), exposing himself to mosquitoes.

12. Wang Siang, thawing the ice to catch carp.

13. The story of Kwoh K'ü, who "is said to have lived in the second century A. D., and to have had an aged mother to support,

besides his own wife and children. Finding that he had not food sufficient for all, he proposed to his wife that they should bury their infant child in order to have the more for their mother's wants; and this devotedness was rewarded by his discovering, while engaged in digging a pit for this purpose, a bar of solid gold which placed him above the reach of poverty, and upon which were inscribed the words: 'A gift from Heaven to Kwoh K'ü; let none deprive him of it!' " (No. 303, p. 95.)

14. Yang Hiang offering himself to the tiger. (No. 882, p. 266.)

15. Cho Show-ch'ang searched fifty years for his mother who had been divorced from his father. Having succeded in his purpose he served her the rest of her life. (No. 81, pp. 26-27.)

16. Yü K'ien-low, ministering unto his sick father. (No. 950, p. 286.)

17. Lao Lai-Tze plays like a child with his parents who suffer from senile childishness.

18. The same story is told of Ts'ai Shun as of Tsêng Shên, viz., that he was recalled from a distance by a sensation of pain which visited him when his mother bit her own finger. During the troubles ensuing upon Wang Mang's usurpation, A. D., 25, when a state of famine prevailed, he nourished his mother with wild berries, retaining only the unripe ones for his own sustenance. On her death, while mourning beside her coffin, he was called away by attendants who exclaimed that the house was on fire; but he refused to leave the spot, and his dwelling remained unharmed. As his mother had been greatly alarmed, in her lifetime, whenever thunder was heard, he made it his duty, after death, to repair to her grave during thunderstorms, and to cry out: "Be not afraid, mother, I am here!" (No. 752, p. 226.) Our illustration depicts him meeting a hunter in the woods who gives him a piece of venison.

19. Huang Hiang, fanning his father's bed.

20. Kiang She in conjunction with his wife devoted himself to waiting upon his aged mother, in order to gratify whose fancy he went daily a long distance to draw drinking water from a river and to obtain fish for her table. This devotedness was rewarded by a miracle. A spring burst forth close by his dwelling, and a pair of

carp were daily produced from it to supply his mother's wants. (No. 256, p. 81.)

21. Wang Ngai comforting the spirit of his mother in a thunder-storm.

22. Ting Lan "flourished under the Han dynasty. After his

mother's death he preserved a wooden effigy representing her figure, to which he offered the same forms of respect and duty as he had observed toward his parent during life. One day, while he was absent from home, his neighbor Chang Shuh came to borrow some household article, whereupon his wife inquired by the divining-slips whether the effigy would lend it, and received a negative reply. Hereupon the neighbor angrily struck the wooden figure. When Ting Lan returned to his home he saw an expression of displeasure on the features of his mother's effigy, and on learning from his wife what had passed, he took a stick and beat the aggressor severely. When he was apprehended for this deed the figure was seen to shed tears, and facts thus becoming known he received high honors from the State." (No. 670, p. 204.)

23. Meng Sung reaping bamboo shoots for his mother in winter.

24. Hwang T'ing-Kien (a celebrated poet of the Sung dynasty), performs menial services in ministering to his parents. (No. 226, p. 73.)

Some of the stories seem silly to us: a pickax would have done better service in breaking the ice than the method of thawing it up with one's own body and catching cold; a mosquito-net would have proved more useful than feeding the insects with the blood of a devoted child, etc. Moreover the stolidity of parents in accepting sacrifices of children with equanimity and as a matter of course is to our sense of propriety nothing short of criminal. Still, it will be wise for us whose habits of life suffer from the opposite extreme, viz., irreverence for authority or tradition in any form, to recognise that all of them are pervaded with a noble spirit of respect for parents, which though exaggerated is none the less touching and ought to command our admiration.